The God of Philosophy

an introduction to the philosophy of religion

Roy Jackson

Published in 2001 by
TPM (The Philosophers' Magazine)
98 Mulgrave Road
Sutton
Surrey
SM2 6LZ

Email: editor@philosophers.co.uk
www.philosophers.co.uk

A catalogue record for this book is
available from the British Library

ISBN 0 9537611-1-8

Printed in Great Britain by
Bookcraft Limited

Contents

*To my wife, Asmi, for her understanding
and support during the writing of this
book, and to my young son, Raef, for his
welcome distractions.*

INTRODUCTION

"Whoever attempts to demonstrate the existence of God…is an excellent subject for a comedy of higher lunacy."
(Søren Kierkegaard, *Philosophical Fragments*)

Does God exist?

Why attempt to prove that God either exists or does not exist? If you are a religious believer then it is more than likely that you do not require an argument to support your belief. If you are a non-believer, then it is highly unlikely that you will convert on the basis of any of the arguments presented in this book. Ultimately the existence of God cannot be *proven* one way or the other. Undoubtedly the most important question that this book needs to address is *not* whether these arguments prove that God exists, but whether it is possible to produce an argument that at least can show that belief can be a *credible and rational* stance to adopt. It may, in fact, be argued that rationality has nothing to do with belief in God. I say this because of what the Danish philosopher **Søren Kierkegaard** (1813-1855) states in the quote above, for although he believed that any attempts to prove the existence of God were foolish, he was a religious believer himself despite his own admission that it was irrational and paradoxical. In itself this is an 'argument': reason cannot prove that God exists, but *faith alone* is sufficient.

The question of whether or not God exists is one you may well have asked yourself, or others, at some stage in your life. You may well have come to the conclusion that God does indeed exist, that you have a certain and clear idea of God, and that you are comfortable and confident in your beliefs. On the other hand, you may believe in God but you may not be altogether clear what 'believing in God' actually means or entails and you might feel that your beliefs are on somewhat shaky foundations. Perhaps you prefer to leave the question open: you do not know whether God exists or not, and so you do not entirely disbelieve in His existence, but nor do you commit yourself to a belief in God. However, you may also be a vehement disbeliever; prepared to argue your case against the existence of any God of any kind and reject all religious belief as a waste of time.

Whatever your viewpoint, the arguments for and against the existence of a God are significant. It is not merely a theological question, but a *philosophical* one. When someone believes in the existence of God, he or she may well be defending a particular doctrinal viewpoint. For example, the Christian, Muslim, Jew or Sikh would defend belief in one God (**monotheism**) and would also believe that the rituals and practises associated with their belief help people to come closer to God. This book is not concerned with the specific rituals and practices of religious believers, but rather the *consequences and implications* of their beliefs. To say that you believe in a God that watches over and protects you raises many questions: What kind of God do you believe in? How does this God watch over you? What are God's intentions if you are harmed in some way? How does this belief affect your outlook on life and the way you live it? Why do you believe in God but someone else does not? Who is right and who is wrong? Is there such a thing as 'right' and 'wrong'?

A word to the wise

Philosophy of religion is a very varied and complex discipline, and there is a need to be very clear in your definitions and terminology. However, many religious believers (I will often use the term 'theists' for brevity) would uphold the view that the sceptical philosopher is simply barking up the wrong tree by pinning down the theist and asking for 'definitions, definitions' as if that were all religious belief was about. It is a common misunderstanding that belief in God somehow rests upon the strength of the arguments for the existence of God. Undoubtedly, the arguments can strengthen (or, alternatively weaken) a belief and it is very important to be able to support your beliefs. However, belief in the existence of God does not rest upon philosophical speculation alone.

Further, no one argument should be seen in isolation: they are not meant to be remote, self-contained 'proofs' that God does or does not exist. Rather, they should be seen as a *whole*, borrowing from each other and being part of a much broader philosophical and theological tradition. In fact, some defer from using the term 'proof' altogether, preferring such phrases as 'more convincing', 'more coherent', 'a stronger defence', 'just as credible' and so forth.

My aim in writing this is primarily to address an audience who are interested in the subject – whether they are studying in a formal way, or just plain interested – but do not necessarily have an axe to grind. It is a book as much for the non-believer as the believer. As a philosopher, my main interest is to examine the structure and implications of each of the arguments for and against the existence of God; their strengths and their weaknesses, their historical contexts and significance. It is an intellectual enterprise that arouses my curiosity. However, it is also an important subject, I believe, because of its implications.

You will note that those who write on the subject of the philosophy of religion tend to belong to one branch or other of Christianity as opposed to other religions. This is largely for historical reasons in that the subject has for a long time been of interest to the Christian tradition, especially as much of its heritage rests within the Ancient Greek philosophical tradition. In this way, philosophy and religion have long been bedfellows and it was not seen as 'un-Christian' to engage in philosophical speculation on theological questions. With certain other religious traditions this has been less the case. Although the same arguments lend themselves to the other great monotheistic traditions such as Judaism and Islam, neither of these traditions – despite having strong philosophical elements – has laid such a great emphasis on arguments for the existence of God as the Christian tradition. Consequently, this text sticks largely within the boundaries of Christian discourse on the topic, although many of the arguments can be applied to at least the other monotheistic traditions. Concerning the so-called Eastern religions, I remain largely silent. Again, to bring in the theologies of Buddhism and Hinduism, for example, would present a whole series of complex, though interesting, arguments that a book of this length could not do justice to.

Apart from concentrating largely, though not exclusively, on the Christian, European philosophical background, this text also restricts itself to what some might regard as a rather traditional approach to the philosophy of religion. It is often argued that much of modern-day discourse on the philosophy of religion is little concerned with the arguments for and against the existence of God, preferring to consider such arguments as exhausted and best laid to rest. Apart from the fact that this view is not at all accurate, I feel that the arguments have had such an historical impact on the philosophy of religion that it would be foolhardy, not to mention careless, to ignore them. It is also the case that, if you study the subject, you will soon discover that the arguments are still a central part of any philosophy of religion course. Further, the arguments are, in my opinion anyway, still very interesting and enjoyable. I sincerely hope you reach the same conclusion.

Chapter One
THE CONCEPT OF GOD

'The fault lies not with God, but with the soul that makes the choice.'

(Plato, *The Republic*)

Before we consider the various arguments for and against the existence of God, we need to have some appreciation of the historical, philosophical and theological understanding of the term 'God'. This is important, as the understanding of God will have obvious implications in terms of defending his existence. What is also significant in terms of the philosophy of religion is the massive impact Greek philosophy has had on Christian belief.

1. THE GOD OF THE GREEKS
1.1 Plato

Plato is one of the founding fathers of Western philosophy and he has had a massive impact on religious and philosophical thought. He lived from around 427-347 BC, spending most of his life in Athens. Plato founded the Academy in Athens and this institution has often been described as the first European university. Here people studied works in philosophy, politics, mathematics, theology, and the sciences for nearly a thousand years.

The importance of Plato's philosophy for religious belief cannot be underestimated. As we shall see, some of the greatest Christian thinkers were familiar with the teachings of Plato, and his works were also translated into Arabic where they were a powerful force in Islamic philosophy.

However, there is another important philosopher that we should mention who was alive before Plato. At around twenty years of age, Plato met a remarkable man: Socrates. As Socrates himself wrote nothing down, what we know of his teachings is mainly through Plato's works.

The main (though by no means *only*) concern for Socrates was morality. Whereas Socrates believed in absolute standards, there were a group of itinerant teachers who thought the opposite: the **Sophists**. The greatest Sophist of all, Protagoras, famously declared that "Man is the measure of all things". By that he meant that it was mankind that established what is right or wrong, not the gods or the existence of a morality independent of man. In other words there is no such thing as an absolute morality, rather it is relative to the individual, the period or the society. This, of course, has important implications for our knowledge of things. If morality is relative, then it is impossible to say that one thing is 'good' and another is 'bad'. For example, the practice of slavery was seen as quite acceptable for the ancient Greeks (it wasn't even perceived as a moral issue) whereas, in our society, it is considered an immoral practice. We would like to believe that our morality is more 'enlightened' in this respect, but to suggest such a thing implies that there is a 'good' morality and a 'bad' morality; that to return to the practice of slavery would be regressive. However, if there is no such thing as an absolute moral standard, then you cannot either 'regress' or 'progress'; it is just a relative matter.

Socrates considered this implication, that there can be no moral standards, as simply unacceptable. There *must be* standards, there *must be* such a thing as a moral Truth. This was effectively Socrates' mission in life: to 'interrogate' the man in the street, to get them to question their beliefs and subject them to philosophic scrutiny in order to determine what ultimately is right and wrong.

During Socrates' latter years his beloved city of Athens was in decline. Its arch-enemy, the militaristic state Sparta, defeated it in 405 BC. This proved to be a massive blow to its confidence and the belief in itself as the mightiest and most sophisticated city-state in Greece. It led the people of Athens to question what had gone wrong and to look for a scapegoat. Led, no doubt, by the politicians who sought power by following the prejudices and passions of the masses, the blame was directed towards Socrates. Athens, seeking security and identity, returned to its old traditions and saw in Socrates the man who most publicly questioned the beliefs in the gods and the old ways, as well as corrupting the youth with his disruptive ideas. As a result Socrates was arrested and was compelled to drink the poison hemlock as his method of execution.

When Socrates was executed Plato was only 29 years old. Plato was a student, indeed, a disciple, of Socrates, and the belief that there are such things as eternal truths was something that Plato took much further than the topic of morality. He believed that *all knowledge* is eternal.

The analogy of the cave
One reason why Plato has remained so popular after so many years is that he was aware of his audience. He wrote mostly in

the form of a dialogue, with Socrates as the main character, and so the reader feels that he is experiencing an unfolding drama. Plato appreciated the importance of explaining often-difficult concepts in a way that could be more readily understood. To achieve this, Plato would make use of **analogy**. An analogy is a way of comparing one thing with another to help bring out their similarity. For example, comparing the structure of an atom to the solar system helps you get a better (though inaccurate) image of how an atom is made up. Perhaps Plato's best-known example of this form is the Analogy of the Cave.

This analogy is from Plato's work the *Republic*. As usual in Plato's dialogues, Socrates is the main character. It is Socrates who asks his fellow conversers to imagine a cave. Deep down at the bottom of this cave are a group of prisoners who are firmly shackled so that they cannot move or turn their heads. They can face in one direction only – the wall of the cave. These prisoners have been in this condition since they were very young children and so the wall of the cave is the only life they have known. Behind the prisoners there is a fire, and between this fire and the prisoners there are many people walking by carrying artificial objects such as wooden figures of men and animals. A screen hides these people walking by, so that only the objects they are carrying appear above the screen. The fire casts a shadow of these objects onto the wall that the prisoners can see. The prisoners are not aware of what is happening behind them and so, for them, the whole of their reality consists of the shadows cast upon the wall of the cave. Even the voices of the people walking behind them they interpret as coming from the shadows.

However, Socrates then tells of one of the prisoners who is freed from his chains and is forced to turn around, look and walk toward the fire and the people. The released prisoner naturally finds all this confusing and painful; the light of the fire is dazzling, the people like some strange creatures from another planet. The prisoner wants only to return to the safe and secure world that he has known, but he is then dragged further upwards towards the entrance of the cave. Exposed to the outside world, the prisoner is unable to adjust to the daylight. Only over time does he gradually grow used to it, first by perceiving the lights of the night sky, then the shadows of objects cast by the sun, and finally the objects themselves in broad daylight. In time, the released prisoner is even able to gaze at the sun itself. By being able to perceive the sun, the prisoner realises it is the source of all things; it is the cause of the changing of the seasons and the giving of life.

Forced to experience the world outside, the prisoner undergoes a gradual awakening; an awareness that there is a more beautiful and real world that is so very different from the dark and superficial world that he has known all his life and was previously so keen to return to. The prisoner also realises that all the things he previously felt were so important no longer matter and are all illusions. What, asks Socrates, would happen if the prisoner then returns to the world of the cave and tells the prisoners what he has seen? Would they welcome him and want to see this world for themselves? On the contrary, the other prisoners would think he had gone mad, for he would not be able to make out the shadows anymore and would come across as a bumbling fool. If the released prisoner attempted to release them by force they would threaten him and even kill him if they had to.

The theory of the Forms

The curious tale of the cave works on many levels. What is it meant to teach us? On one level, the audience of the time would have recognised the released prisoner as Socrates himself: the man who dared to question the conventions of his time; the man who claimed that there was a greater, better, truer world beyond the trivia of everyday life; the man who ultimately had to pay with his life for forcing others to question those things they held so dear. On another level, the released prisoner is every philosopher; anyone who searches for truth and sees it as their mission in life to teach this truth to others, regardless of the dangers.

At another level, however, the analogy of the cave is Plato's way of explaining the **Theory of the Forms**. What are these 'Forms'? The French poet and writer Antoine de Saint-Exupéry recounts in his book *The Little Prince* how, as a child, he lived in a house where there was supposed to be some buried treasure. The treasure, of course, was never found but it was the *possibility* that it might exist that gave the house a magical quality. As Saint-Exupéry says, "What is essential is invisible to the eye." This is what Plato also meant by the Forms; they are the 'essential' things that are invisible to the eye or our other senses.

In the *Republic,* Plato points out that the analogy is a picture of the human condition. People are trapped within the illusory world of the senses like the prisoners at the bottom of the cave. However, Plato believed that it is possible to escape from this illusion and to perceive the truth that exists within our very souls. For example, we can see many beautiful things: a beautiful sunset, a beautiful person, a beautiful flower. But what is *beauty itself*? How do we know that so many different kinds of objects share the attribute of 'beauty'? For Plato, we know what beauty is because there exists a 'form' of beauty; beauty itself. In fact, *everything* has a form; a table, a tree, a horse.

For Plato, the Forms represent truth, or reality. They cannot be attained by the senses (touch, taste, smell, sight, or hearing), but through the exercise of the mind. However, these Forms are *independent* of the mind: they are eternal, unchanging and perfect. Our knowledge of the Forms is innate, contained within our very souls, and so when we perceive them we are recollecting our knowledge of the Forms, of truth.

Plato and religion

For Plato, therefore, there are two realms. There is the visible realm, that is the world of matter, of the senses, of change, the world in which everything is always becoming something else, the world where everything is imperfect and subject to decay. However, there is the other realm, the intelligible realm in which there is perfection, permanence and order. This is the unchanging, the timeless realm. It is reality. The implications of the existence of these two realms is that man is faced with a choice: To live a life 'in the shadows', living an animal existence and pursuing pleasures and prizes that are temporal and fleeting; or to exercise our powers of reason and achieve awareness of the eternally good and beautiful. The latter option is the most difficult, for it requires self-discipline, a denial of sensual pleasures and the temptations of the world. Plato saw the weaknesses of the body as an 'evil' that gets in the way of the pursuits of the mind. Bodily pleasures and desires hinder the progress of the eternal soul in its journey towards the realm of the Forms.

All of this will be familiar to many religious believers, especially within the Christian tradition. This is no coincidence. In many respects, the Bible of the Jews – the Hebrew Scriptures – is very different from what became the New Testament. Early Christianity developed its doctrines within the Roman Empire; a society that was culturally bound to Greek philosophy. St. Paul, the man who more than any other promoted and developed Christian thought, was born a Jew, educated a Greek, and raised as a Roman citizen. To make Christianity accessible and understandable to the Roman mind, it was necessary to incorporate Greek thought within it. Socrates and Plato were considered 'Christians before Christ'; they paved the way for the coming of Christianity by providing it with philosophical and theoretical foundations that would be acceptable to the western mind.

In the analogy of the cave, the sun represents the Form of the Good. In the same way that the sun is the source of all things and gives light to them, the Form of the Good is over and above the other Forms, giving them light and allowing us to perceive them. Therefore, when you have awareness of the Form of the Good you have achieved true enlightenment. In Christianity, the Form of the Good becomes God: the source of all things.

1.2 Aristotle
The nature of being

Aristotle (384-322 BC) was a student of Plato's at the Academy. However, he later criticised Plato's Forms because he could not see how such things could exist, or what possible evidence there is for their existence. Plato, for example, argued that there is a Form for our morals, that is there is a Form for justice so that, when we can perceive the Forms, we will know what to do in moral situations. Aristotle, however, believed that morality is such a changeable thing that it is impossible for something like a Form, so unchangeable and universal, to be applied to everyday situations.

A crucial question for Aristotle was, 'what is being?' Aristotle was raising an important and interesting problem here. We can accept that the whole universe is made up of 'stuff' or 'matter'. But how does this matter, this raw material of the universe, become existing things? How does a pile of matter 'turn into' a planet, a sun, a tree, an animal? What gives things their being?

For Plato, 'being' resides in the realm of the Forms. Raw matter is turned into things through the artistry of the 'Demiurge', the divine creator. In Christianity, God is the grand artisan, the designer and builder. However, Aristotle believed that we should look to *this world* for the nature of things. For example, what makes a car what it is? It is not simply the material – the metal, the glass, the rubber, the plastic, and so on that makes it a car – if you were to buy a car and it was delivered to your door as a heap of unconnected materials you would not be too happy. Rather, what makes a car what it is – what gives it being – is its structure or its form. For Plato, there is a Form of a horse. For Aristotle, the form lies *within* the species of horse, not outside of it.

The four causes

If we are not prepared to accept that there is a grand designer of some kind that gives things their form, then we are led down the path of materialism. That is, all that exists is matter and nothing else. However, the problem here is how can matter become something? What is the *motivating force* behind, or within matter that causes it to form into a tree or an animal? For Aristotle there are four related causes for the existence of things. For example, there are four causes of a tree's existence:

The material cause. For a tree to be a tree it must have the raw material: the bark, the leaves and so on.

The formal cause. Just having the raw materials is not enough for it to be a tree. It must also have a specific structure that is unique to it – that which causes it to be an oak tree rather than a cedar tree.

The efficient cause. This is what makes it become a tree in its particular environment; for example, the soil, the sun, the rain and so on. In other words, the tree is being 'pushed' by external causes in a certain direction.

The final cause. For Aristotle all things are aiming towards a specific end, a '***telos***' or 'purpose'. This is the final cause. In the case of the tree its final cause is to be an adult tree!

So, for Aristotle, all things are striving towards a final condition and all things are limited by this. For example, a tree cannot become an antelope, nor a fish become a bird. The important point is that the forms of things are contained *within* nature, they are not some supernatural, mystical, magical force. Everything has a form and matter is the potentiality of form. All things have both **potentiality** and **actuality.** For example, adult man is the actuality of which the child was the potentiality; the child is the actuality of which the embryo is the potentiality; the embryo the actuality of which the ovum was the potentiality and so on.

Aristotle sees nature as a battleground between chaotic, formless matter and the inner necessity, the shaping force that moulds material into specific figures and purpose, the realisation of its potentiality. When there are faults in nature then it is because matter has resisted the powers of the forming process. And so everything is guided in a certain direction – the egg towards a chicken, the acorn towards an oak – but this is not an external providence but a natural cause.

Up until this point Aristotle would be in line with much modern scientific thinking. However, Aristotle raises the question, what started it all? How did the inert, eternal matter start the process of becoming in the first place? Although matter might have no beginning, it is inconceivable that motion also has no beginning and, for Aristotle, all things are in motion, moving from potentiality to actuality. Motion must have a source, a **Prime Mover**. This Prime Mover, or Unmoved Mover, is incorporeal, indivisible, spaceless, sexless, changeless, perfect, and eternal. He is not a creator God, but a mechanical force that moves all things. Again, this 'Mover' might not seem so far removed from modern physics if this 'God' is so abstract as to be a pure magnetic force. However, Aristotle says that God has *self-consciousness* . But what does this God do? Seemingly nothing, for it has no passions or desires, it is *pure actuality* and so has no potential to become anything else, or to act in any way. It has put the world into motion and now has no more role to play. Its only occupation is to contemplate the essence of things and as He Himself is the essence of things, then He contemplates Himself!

The Aristotelian God is far removed from the personal, acting God of the Jews or the loving, fatherly God of the Christians. However, Aristotle's views on motion, cause and purpose had a huge influence on Christian scholars, notably **St. Thomas Aquinas** (1225-1274). In the teleological argument (see Chapter Three), Aquinas adopted Aristotle's belief that motion must have a beginning, which he took to be God. Further, Aquinas also addressed the question of if all things have a potentiality, what then is man's full potential? This affected Aquinas' ethics and his belief that Man has the potential to reflect God's nature and goodness.

2. THE GOD OF CLASSICAL THEISM

Much philosophy of religion, as traditionally understood, rests within the European Christian tradition. It is therefore not surprising that it presents a particular view of God. What we mean when we talk about God is extremely important from the outset, as the arguments tend to rely upon a particular conception of God.

The religious believer is sometimes referred to as a **theist**. The term **'theism'** can mean a belief in a god or gods. However, in Christianity, theism usually refers to the 'classical' concept of God, as elaborated by St. Thomas Aquinas and most commonly understood by mainstream Christianity today. Briefly, God is perceived as single, omnipotent (all-powerful), omniscient (all-knowing), and omnibenevolent (all-good). This is also the orthodox view for Jews and Muslims.

2.1 God is single

There are no other gods, but God. This is a belief in a single (*monos*) God, and is referred to as **monotheism**. There are a number of other 'theisms':

Polytheism. A belief in the existence of many (*poly*) gods. This was a belief held by ancient Greeks, the Romans and Egyptians. It is also a belief held by a number of religions today, such as forms of Hinduism.

Pantheism. The belief that God is everything (*pan*). That is, God is not separate from the world but *is* the world. All things are God. Within most great religious traditions there are groups who believe this. A number of Christians today, known as **process theologians**, speak of **panentheism**, the belief that God is so much a part of the world that He is affected by it. When we suffer, God suffers (see Chapter Ten).

Henotheism. Also a belief in many gods, but one (*henos*) rules above all others. Early references to the Biblical God talk of Him competing with other Gods for supremacy.

Atheism. A disbelief in the existence of God or gods. This view can be an outright rejection of religious belief, or a position maintaining a large degree of scepticism. Atheism can also be found within religious belief, however. For example, many Buddhists consider themselves atheists.

Agnosticism. This holds that we can never be certain one way or the other whether God exists or not. There have been a number of different forms of agnosticism throughout history and it is possible (though psychologically difficult) to be a religious agnostic in the sense that a person may have faith but does not see this as providing *knowledge* of God in any way.

2.2 God is personal

For many people today, a belief in a personal God may be understood in terms of a 'force' or an 'absolute' of some kind. Within Classical Theism, however, God is frequently **anthropomorphised**: that is, He is spoken of in human, personal terms. God is not an 'it' but a 'He' (within the Classical definition, the term 'She' is not generally used), and the language used concerning God's actions and attributes are also couched in human terms: God loves, God is kind, God is wise, God sits upon His throne, God walks with Adam in the Garden of Eden, etc. Such use of human language raises problems, as it does seem to humanise God to too great a degree.

2.3 God is All

The Greek word 'omni' means 'all' or 'everything'. For the Classical Theist, God is:

Omnipotent. From the Greek *potens* (able). God, being God, is able to do everything. God cannot be limited in any way, for then he would not be the greatest being. However, there are problems in that it is not clear what is meant by 'everything'. For example, can God make a square circle, or kill Himself, or create a being greater than Himself, or produce an immovable object and then move it? Classical Theism tends to adopt the view that God is able to do *possible* things which are *consistent* with nature. Further, omnipotence does not mean that God is some vicious tyrant, inflicting trial and tribulation upon whomever He wishes. God is identified with the Greek word **agapé** (love), for He is concerned only with the welfare of His creation. However, this seems to conflict with the fact that there is so much evil and suffering in the world (See Chapter Ten).

Omniscient. From the Greek word *sciens* (knowing). God is all-knowing. God does not only know all there is to know in the present, but also the past *and* the future. He can reveal this future to select people, such as prophets. In fact, to talk of God as even existing in time is regarded by many theologians as a mistake: for God there is no past, present and future. God is **timeless**. God does not exist within time, for time is also a creation of God and He cannot be governed or be a part of it. Also, God must be **spaceless** in that he does not exist within space, as this is also His creation. As God is not in any way affected by time or space, He also is not subject to change, he is **immutable** (changeless) and, of course, **immortal** (cannot die). Some philosophers and theologians have argued that an infallible God who knows all that is to occur in the future is incompatible with the belief that human beings can have free will. For example, if God already knows that I will write this book, then I have no choice but to write it. Some scholars have attempted to get around the problem of free will by arguing that God is **eternal**, or **everlasting**: that is, He lives forever but *within* time. In this sense, God does not know the future because it has not happened yet. However, this places a limit upon his omniscience and his omnipotence.

Omnipresent. God is not only present at *any* place, but also at *every* place at the same time. The theologian **St. Anselm**, (c. 1033-1109) wrote that "the Supreme Being exists in every place and at all times," then later said that God, "exists in no place and at no time." These do seem contradictory statements, but Anselm is attempting to get round the difficulty of using everyday language such as 'place' and 'time' in terms of a timeless and spaceless God. God cannot be circumscribed by place or time so, in that sense, He cannot be *in it*. God is 'present' in the sense that all things are subject to God's power and knowledge.

Omnibenevolent. God is all-good. He is not an evil God, and nor is he the creator of evil (for a further elaboration of this and the problems with it, see Chapter Ten). Rather, God *is* goodness, for goodness is not something separate from God. God is, therefore, a moral God and represents moral perfection. Humankind, for its part, can share in this by aiming to also be good.

Further reading

Jackson, Roy, *Plato: A Beginner's Guide*, Hodder & Stoughton, 2001.

Stump, Eleanor & Michael J. Murray (ed), *Philosophy of Religion: The Big Questions*, Blackwell, 1999. (Chaps. 1-7)

Quinn, Philip L. and Charles Taliaferro, *A Companion to Philosophy of Religion*, Blackwell, 1999. (Chaps. 27-40)

Thompson, Mel, *Teach Yourself Philosophy of Religion*, Hodder & Stoughton, 1997. (Chap.3)

Vardy, Peter, *The Puzzle of God*, Fount, 1999 edition. (Chaps. 1-3)

Chapter Two
THE COSMOLOGICAL ARGUMENT

"Nothing will come of nothing."
(William Shakespeare, *King Lear*)

The term 'cosmological' derives from two Greek words: *'kosmos'* and *'logos'*. *'Kosmos'* is translated into English as 'cosmos' and is synonymous with 'universe', whereas *'logos'* means 'blueprint' or 'plan'. And so, 'cosmology' refers to the 'blueprint of the universe'. It is hardly surprising that the term has a Greek derivation, because, as we have seen, the origins and make-up of the universe were a pre-occupation for many Greek philosophers. Modern-day cosmologists (those who study the nature and origins of the universe) tend to be scientists, but most religious traditions also possess a cosmology.

The reason the first argument for the existence of God that we will look at is called the cosmological argument is because it begins by looking at the 'blueprint' of the universe and then goes on to conclude that the nature of the universe suggests that there must be a God. This might seem to you to be a giant leap to make, and so we need to consider carefully the steps taken in reaching such a conclusion.

The cosmological argument is sometimes referred to as the **'causal argument'** or the **'first cause argument'** and this should give you some indication as to what is at the heart of the argument. Following on from the fact that there is a universe it seems perfectly justified in asking *why* is there a universe? The main difficulty, of course, is what we can be sure of when we talk of the origins of the universe and this is really where views differ. For the theist the origin of the universe lies with a creator God. For the non-theist, other explanations must be given or, as we shall see in some cases, no explanation at all is required.

One thing you will soon become aware of, incidentally, is that the philosophy of religion makes use of quite a number of Greek and Latin terms. You have already come across some Greek (*kosmos* and *logos*), but it will help to also be familiar with the Latin **'a priori'** and **'a posteriori'**. You might probably be able to determine roughly the meaning of these two terms because of similar words in English: 'prior' and 'posterior'. The cosmological argument, together with the argument in the next chapter (the teleological argument), are *'a posteriori'*; that is, they argue for the existence of God *after* ('posterior to') considering various facts about the world. We know from experience that there is a universe, and we can make certain assertions about the nature of this universe and so, from there, it is hoped we can then reach some conclusions as to its origins. We will also be looking at the ontological argument in Chapter Four, which is *'a priori'*; it concludes that there must be a God *before* even considering our experience of the universe. In other words, it makes use of our powers of thought and reason, *not* experience.

Another point to bear in mind: there are different versions of the cosmological argument, and below we will consider how some of these differ from one another.

1. THE KALAM COSMOLOGICAL ARGUMENT

The term *'kalam'* is Arabic, and is probably best translated as 'speech', though more specifically it relates to discussing theological issues that arise from belief in the Muslim faith. The term is distinguished from *falsafa* (Arabic for 'philosophy') in that *kalam* starts from the basis that Islam is the truth and then goes on to use philosophical tools to defend its claims, whereas *falsafa* emphasises reason, sometimes at the expense of faith. The group belonging to the *kalam* was part of the intellectual movement known as **scholasticism**. Briefly, scholasticism was a movement that dominated the universities of Europe from the eleventh to the fifteenth centuries and was an attempt to integrate reason (notably that of ancient Greek philosophy) with religion. Between the tenth and twelfth centuries, Muslim philosophers residing in Spain, which was part of the Muslim empire at the time, dominated the scholastic debate. One person who has studied the *Kalam* cosmological argument extensively is the modern philosopher **William L. Craig** who wrote, "Probably no chapter in the history of the cosmological argument is as significant – or as universally ignored – as that of the Arabic theologians and philosophers." He wrote that over twenty years ago now, but the situation has not improved much.

Although the basis for the cosmological argument lies with Greek philosophy, it was really the Muslim philosophers of the Middle Ages who generated the debate to any great extent. The *kalam* group consisted of such notable Muslim philosophers as **al-Kindi** (died c. 870) and **al-Ghazali** (1058-1111). One of their important contributions was to consider the origins of the universe and the difficulties involving the idea that the universe has existed forever, for infinity. Infinity is riddled with conceptual difficulties. Al-Ghazali stated that no **actual infinities** could exist. That is to say, we can talk of a **potential infinity,** such as an infinite series of numbers, but this is very different from them existing in *actuality* (i.e. in the 'real world').

An actual infinity would result in unacceptable logical paradoxes. For example, you can conceive of a library with an infinite number of books, but what would happen if you then add another ten books? Can you have infinity *plus* ten? In other words, can infinity *grow?* **Zeno of Elea** (5th century BCE) presented a number of famous brain-teasers involving the idea of infinity. For example, the Greek hero Achilles engages in a race with a tortoise. To give him an advantage, the tortoise is given a head-start. However, according to Zeno, Achilles can never overtake the tortoise: when he reaches the point at which the tortoise began, the tortoise will have moved forward to another position, and when Achilles reaches that point, the tortoise will again have moved to another position, and so on. Similarly, an arrow can never reach its target: when it is fired it can reach half-way towards its target, then half-way again, then half-way of that, and so on. In other words, the distance between the archer and the target is infinitely divisible. However, we know that in *actuality* the arrow does reach its target, and so these are examples of potential infinites.

These are just some examples of the problems encountered when we attempt to bring the concept of infinity into the debate. There have been more recent attempts to resolve the problem of actual and potential infinities, for example from the mathematician **Georg Cantor** (1845-1918) who, through his **theory of sets**, argued that infinity does have an actual existence. But these have also been criticised.

The *Kalam* argument can be presented as a series of points:

1. Actual infinity is not possible
2. Therefore, if you trace the series of causes for the existence of the universe back in time this cannot go on for infinity
3. The universe must have begun at a certain moment in time
4. This moment in time is the cause of the universe
5. The cause of the universe is God

We will consider later why we might reach the conclusion that the cause must be God. Suffice to say for now that for philosophers such as Al-Ghazali any agent that was capable of causing the creation of something as complex and immense as the universe must deserve the title of 'God'. The question that might come to mind, however, is why such a causer must be perceived as a *personal agent*. However, at the very least, it does raise the interesting question as to what could cause the universe to exist and, indeed, if there must be a first cause at all.

2. THOMAS AQUINAS

The Christian theologian and philosopher St. Thomas Aquinas was a product of the scholastic movement, and it is worthwhile spending some time on him in this chapter as he presents the most famous version of the cosmological argument. Aquinas, incidentally, adopted the stance of the *kalam* group that actual infinity is impossible

Between 1265-73, Aquinas wrote *Summa Theologica* ('*Summary Treatise of Theology*') in which he presented his famous **'Five Ways'**. Basically, each 'way' is an argument – or what Aquinas termed a '***demonstratio***' – that begins with a fact that we can observe. He then reaches a conclusion that is not subject to everyday observation. The ways below should help to illustrate how this process works.

Whereas Aquinas' 'Fifth Way' can be seen as a version of the teleological argument (see Chapter Three), the cosmological argument is summed up in his First, Second and Third Ways. (The 'Fourth Way', incidentally, relates to the moral argument which will be considered in Chapter Five.) As they are three separate 'ways' they are actually three arguments that complement each other, or perhaps it is better to say that they are three parts of the same argument. And so, although they are usually put together, there are subtle differences that need to be made clear.

Before introducing his Five Ways, Aquinas stated this important caveat:

> "God's effects ... are enough to prove that God exists, even if they are not enough to help us comprehend what he is."(Thomas Aquinas, *Summa Theologica*)

Aquinas believed that his Five Ways might show us that God exists, but it cannot tell us anything about the nature of God; about what God actually is. Therefore, Aquinas would readily agree with the critic who argues that his Five Ways cannot prove the existence of the Christian God (the all-good, omnipotent, omniscient etc). Rather, the aim is to show that there must exist 'something' and this 'something' could be God. As you will see in Chapter Five, the importance that faith plays in the understanding of God should not be ignored, and this is the danger of treating these different arguments as isolated proofs.

2.1 Aquinas' 'First Way': The argument from motion

Aquinas' 'First Way' can be summarised as:

1. In the world, some things are in motion.
2. For something to move, it must be moved by something else.
3. Movement cannot go on for infinity.
4. Therefore, there must be a first mover (God).

Now, we need to consider each of these points very carefully to see just how logical and credible an argument they produce.

1. *In the world, some things are in motion.* As with the other ways, Aquinas starts from an *a posteriori* premise. That is, we can accept this as a fact based upon our experience. There is little to disagree with here. We need, however, to be clear what Aquinas means by 'motion'. For Aquinas it refers to any kind of change, in quantity as well as quality. It need not be a reference to your position in space. For example, you may be sitting in a chair and might argue that you are not 'in motion'. However your body is still undergoing change (ageing, heart-beating, brain-processing, and so on). Even a stone is changing, through erosion by wind and rain etc., however slowly that might be. However, Aquinas did not want to go so far as to say all things are in motion; for example such seemingly universal 'things' as geometrical shapes, and mathematical formulae would not qualify as moving objects.

2. *For something to move, it must be moved by something else.* This view sees the world in its 'natural condition' as being completely still. Therefore, the movement of things is 'unnatural' and must, by extension, be caused by something that is 'supernatural'. In *Summa Theologica*, Aquinas uses such phrases as 'potentiality' and 'actuality', which are essentially borrowings from Aristotle (see Chapter One). Aquinas believed that things are changed by something outside of themselves. For example, a piece of wood (what Aquinas would call an 'actuality') has the *potential* to be a chair, a table, ashes, and so on. So a piece of wood is both actuality (a

piece of wood) and potentiality (a table, for example). However, this potential can be achieved only by, say, something setting fire to the wood to turn it into ashes. It cannot *cause itself* to be set on fire. There has to be an external, causal force. There are limits to potentialities, of course. A piece of wood does not have the potential to be a human being. The only thing that has *pure actuality* is God. God cannot have potential because then He would not be perfect.

3. *Movement cannot go on for infinity.* Even if we accept that (1) and (2) are true, can the same be said of (3)? In terms of motion, imagine the whole universe as a globe you can hold in your hands. You watch it constantly in motion in the same way, say, as you would the operation of an old watch that you have opened up. For the universe to continue to move, you have to shake the globe now and then, rather like you have to wind up a watch. In this sense, you are the mover, the changer; you are outside the universe. Without you, there would be no movement. This, by the way, was the classical view of God adopted by most theologians at the time of Aquinas: not a God that began the process of motion, and then simply sat back or died – like the Aristotelian God – but a God who *continues* to cause motion; rather like a musician who plays music. If the musician dies, or stops playing, then so does his music. Therefore, for there to be *present* motion there has to be an *existing* mover.

4. *Therefore, there must be a first mover (God).* Even if we are prepared to accept the idea that movement cannot continue forever without a first cause and that there must, therefore, be a first mover, it might strike you as a giant leap to conclude that the first mover is God. However, assuming some force or other is capable of causing the whole universe to move while not itself being subject to any external force *would* lead to the conclusion that this force is something of immense power.

2.2 Aquinas' 'Second Way': The argument from efficient cause

This can be summarised as:

1. In the world, events occur.
2. Every event (effect) has a cause
3. It is impossible for a series of causes to be infinite.
4. Therefore, there must be a first cause (God).

At first it may seem that Aquinas has merely substituted the word 'motion' for 'cause.' However, there is a subtle difference between the two that would certainly not have gone unnoticed amongst the diligent medieval scholastics. In the First Way, Aquinas noted that there are things in the world that are undergoing change and reasoned that there must be some ultimate 'changer' or 'mover' that is itself 'unchanged' or 'unmoved'. In the Second Way, Aquinas intends to show that there are things in the world that are caused to exist by other things and then concludes that there must be something whose own existence is uncaused.

Once again, each stage of the argument needs to be examined in order to assess its overall success.

1. *In the world, events occur.* Again, this is a fairly solid *a posteriori* premise: events do indeed occur. Aquinas uses the term 'effects' rather than 'events', but both terms can be used in the same way to indicate that something 'happens': the sun rises, you walk across the road, a bird flies by, a meteor hits the earth, and so on.

2. *Every event (effect) has a cause.* Each event does not happen by itself, but is caused by something else. Suppose, for example, a piano falls from a multi-storey building and misses you by an inch. It would be a little bizarre if you simply continue to walk on with the remark, "oh, these things just happen". At the very least, you might stop and think for a moment *why* this event occurred. But can it be argued that not every event has a cause? Some state that a given electron can pass out of existence and then later return to existence in a different orbit around the nucleus without, it seems, any cause. However, it could well be that science is as yet unable to *determine* the cause, not that there *isn't* a cause.

3. *It is impossible for a series of causes to be infinite.* Like the argument that motion cannot go on for infinity, the belief that an infinite series of causes is impossible is a debatable one. However, you must remember that Aquinas assumed the definition of God as an existing causer.

4. *Therefore, there must be a first cause (God).* A common criticism of this conclusion is that even if we accept that an infinite series of causes is impossible, there seems little reason to suppose that there should only be *one* cause and this must be God.

How does Aquinas' First Cause Argument differ from the *kalam* argument? The fundamental difference is how causation is viewed.

For the *kalam* group, the concern was viewing the causes as a linear process going back in time. In other words, stretching back into the past in a straight line:

A ———→ B ———→ C ———→ D ———→ E etc.

This raises problems if you view time as a circle as then you never reach a first cause:

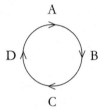

Aquinas, however, viewed causation as a hierarchical process. That is, you can take any event in the present and sketch out a hierarchy of causes going back in time in the following fashion:

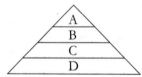

As an example, 'A' could be any event occurring at this moment. For example, you decide to put this book down and feed the cat. That single event (feeding the cat) has a hierarchy of causes. For example, 'B' could be your awareness of the time (time to feed the cat), or the cat meowing at the door. Further on, 'C' could be the causes that led to the cat's existence, or the production of the cat food. 'D' could be the culture of keeping pets. And so on. As you trace the causes the pyramid columns get larger and larger (that is, they grow exponentially) as more and more causes become inter-related to each other until, eventually, you reach a first cause The causes and effects exist simultaneously rather than one after another in a linear fashion. This fits in with Aquinas' view of God: not as a being that committed the initial act of creation and then sat back, but as a being whose continual activity keeps things going. If God were to stop 'causing' – like the musician who stops playing the music – then there would no longer be any effects.

2.3 Aquinas' Third Way: The argument from contingency and necessity

This is a fascinating argument, and is the one most closely associated with the traditional cosmological argument. The third version is sometimes known as the **modal cosmological argu-**

ment. The term 'modality' is a reference to contingency, necessity, possibility and so forth. A **contingent** thing (by 'thing' Aquinas meant just about anything that you can conceive, not just human beings, but tables, chairs, trees, etc.) is, by definition, something that, logically, could not have been. For example, it is logically possible that my parents may not have met when they did, and so I would not now exist. In Aquinas' terms, I have been 'generated' (born at a certain point at time), and I am in the process of becoming 'corrupt' (that is, ageing; this isn't a remark about my moral status!). Therefore, my existence – either in the past, now, or in the future – is by no means guaranteed. I possess the possibility of *not being*, a state I am not, quite frankly, looking forward to. The same could be said of you or this book that you are reading. This book has not always existed – if that had been the case then there would be little point me writing it. Further, its pages will in time yellow and turn to dust. You could certainly attempt to preserve the book – and I would not blame you for wanting to do this – but time will *eventually* take its toll. Also, I may well have decided not to write this book at all, in which case it would not exist now, or I may have chosen to change its content, in which case it would not be the same book.

Aquinas also talks of **necessary beings or things**. Aquinas is careful to point out that not all things are contingent. For example, the existence of geometry, mathematics, and logic are necessary. In other words, they cannot *not* exist, or be any other way than they are. Two plus two *must* equal four. A triangle *must* have three sides. I cannot be four foot tall and six foot tall at the same time.

Having got the terminology clear, we can summarise Aquinas' argument thus:

1. In this world, there are contingent beings/things.
2. If we accept that time is infinite, there must have been a point when there was nothing.
3. If there was once nothing, then there would be nothing now.
4. Therefore, there must be something that is necessary.
5. Every necessary thing is either caused by another, or is not.
6. As the Second Way has shown, causes cannot go on for infinity
7. Therefore, there must be a necessary being that is the cause of itself and not dependent on any other.
8. This we call God.

We must again examine this argument more closely.

1. *In this world, there are contingent beings/things.* Again, we begin with an *a posteriori* fact: contingent beings exist. As already noted, by 'beings' Aquinas is not restricting himself to just human beings, but anything that has a distinct identity. Contingent beings "are possible to be and not to be"; that is that they could either exist or not. The important point about contingent things is that they come into being at a certain time, and also cease to exist at a later time; that is, they have life spans which can vary from milliseconds to millions of years.

2. *If we accept that time is infinite, there must have been a point when there was nothing.* This is on the assumption that all things are contingent. Contingency, it is argued, cannot continue forever. The main difference between Aquinas' Third Way and the previous two ways is that he is prepared to accept that infinity is possible *per se*, but then goes on to show infinite time must require a necessary being. Contingency, logically speaking, cannot continue forever because then it would not be contingent. For example, if you were to add up the lifespan for all the contingent beings and things in the universe and come up with x number of years then, if time is infinite, what existed one year *before* x years, or even one minute, or one second before? Nothing would have existed! So how can you come from nothing existing, to contingent things existing without a necessary being that began the whole process?

3. *If there were once nothing, then there would be nothing now.* This follows from 2. If it has been shown that there must have been a time when there was nothing, then things cannot simply come into existence of their own accord.

4. *Therefore, there must be something that is necessary.* As there are things that exist, then there must have been a necessary being that caused contingent things to exist in the first place. Aquinas believed that there must be a good reason as to *why* things exist. This belief was later re-stated and formulated by the German philosopher **Gottfried Wilhelm Leibniz** (1646-1716). Like Aquinas, and the *kalam* group preceding him, Leibniz believed in what has become known as the **Principle of Sufficient Reason**: there must be a complete explanation for why something exists. In other words, we presuppose in all our rational thinking that everything that exists has a reason for its existence. Aquinas argues that every being is either (a) explained by another being (contingent) or (b) explained by itself (necessary). According to the Principle of Sufficient Reason, it is not possible for a being to be (c) explained by nothing.

5. *Every necessary thing is either caused by another, or is not.* How, you might wonder, can a necessary being be caused at all? Here, Aquinas was making reference to the belief at the time in angels; that is, beings that do not go out of existence but are created by God. Although this section of Aquinas' argument is often omitted in more modern debate, it does raise the issue of whether or not there are other things that might count as caused necessary beings or things. Foe example, did God create numbers, mathematics and so on? In a sense, if God created everything, then all necessary things are caused, except for God.

6. *As the Second Way has shown, causes cannot go on for infinity.* Here Aquinas is dependent upon the proofs demonstrated in the Second Way.

7. *Therefore, there must be a necessary being that is the cause of itself and not dependent on any other. 8. This we call God.* How does Aquinas reach the assumption that a necessary being must exist? This is the crux of the argument: We observe that all contingent beings (you, me, trees, flowers, rocks etc.) have a cause for their existence. It seems a reasonable conclusion to reach, therefore, that if the universe is contingent then it too has a cause. Now, it is quite conceivable – indeed logically possible – that the universe need not have existed at all, therefore it is contingent and, therefore, it has a cause. As the universe cannot cause itself, then the cause of its existence must rest *outside* the universe. This cause Aquinas defines as a necessary being and this, by definition, is God.

3. CRITICISMS

Both Leibniz and Aquinas found the concept of infinity unsatisfactory. Their dissatisfaction was based on the scientific premise that things are not 'just there', but are in some way related to other things. Leibniz, here, is a proponent of the ancient metaphysical thesis **'ex nihilo nihil fit'** ('of nothing, nothing comes'); but this, of course, sits somewhat uncomfortably alongside the belief that God created the universe *ex nihilo* (out of nothing).

Interestingly, however, modern-day cosmologists also talk of the universe coming 'out of nothing'. Here is a modern-day explanation for the existence of the universe: We know that you, as a human being, are a result of sexual reproduction. You are the product of your parents. In fact, the human race as a whole is the result of an evolutionary process. All life forms on Earth are the result of atoms – particularly carbon and oxygen – combining into complex molecules in an environment warmed by a stable sun. Our sun is a middle-aged star and the Earth, together with the rest of the solar system, was formed around 4.5 billion years ago. Our star is just one of an aggregate of stars that make up a galaxy – the Milky Way - which, in turn, is one of an aggregate of galaxies that formed around 10 billion years ago. All the galaxies make up the universe, which began around 15 billion years ago as a result of a **'Big Bang'**. This 'Big Bang' was an explosion that occurred 'out of nothing'. It began with the universe packed into a space smaller than an atomic nucleus that rapidly expanded in a tiny fraction of a second into a dense mixture of radiant energy and exotic particles.

Are you content with this answer? Are you not still justified in asking the inevitable follow-on question: "Yes, but what *caused* the Big Bang?" The cosmologist may go on and speculate on the possibility that the Big Bang is actually a part of a series of such events: the universe expands, then shrinks again and the whole process begins all over *ad infinitum (*i.e. forever). This is known as the **Oscillating Universe Theory**. There may also be other Big Bangs, in which case our universe is part of a *multiverse* (that is, many 'universes'). This theory might counter the suggestion that infinity is impossible.

3.1 Russell vs. Copleston

In 1947 there was an interesting radio debate between **Bertrand Russell** (1872-1970) and **F.C. Copleston** (1907-). Copleston was a Jesuit priest and professor of the History of Philosophy at Heythrop College. Russell, a British philosopher, was always a critic of religious belief, perhaps most evident in his *Why I Am Not a Christian* (1957.) The transcript of the radio debate is printed in that book. There are two main points from the debate that are worth summarising:

1. Why should we accept the Principle of Sufficient Reason? In other words, does there really *have* to be a reason for everything? The Principle of Sufficient Reason, remember, is very closely related to the idea of contingency. This states that if all beings are dependent, then it follows that there must be a necessary being to provide a reason for all this dependency. This necessary being, God, is therefore in a special category of His own. The question that Russell raises, however, is where does this 'special category' come from? Why should we accept that there must be such a category?

Russell said, "I don't admit the idea of a necessary being and I don't admit that there is a particular meaning in calling other beings 'contingent'. These phrases don't for me have a significance except within a logic I reject."

Whereas Russell argues that a 'necessary being' has no meaning, Copleston retorts that by being able to talk about it, Russell understands the meaning of a 'necessary being' (which Coppleston defines as 'a being that must and cannot not-exist'). Basically, by talking about a 'necessary being' you know what is meant by it, therefore you cannot say it is meaningless. People cannot sit around a table and discuss a topic that has no meaning to them!

Inevitably, however, Copleston and Russell talk in circles and have to 'agree to disagree' on this point. As Russell says, "I should say that the universe is just there, that is all." In other words, there is no reason for its existence and it is pointless trying to find a reason. Of course, this is a denial that there has to be a reason for everything and, you may argue, seems a rather un-philosophical conclusion to reach.

2. The second, and closely related, point is the move from the dependency of individual beings to the dependency of the whole universe. Russell says, "Every man who exists has a mother, and it seems to me your argument is that therefore the human race must have a mother, but obviously the human race hasn't a mother..." For Russell, to talk of the cause of the universe *as a whole* is meaningless. For example, I may be able to explain the reasons why a number of people read this book (i.e. what causes you to read this book). Person one may be reading it to help him pass his exam; Person two because she is interested in the subject; Person three because he bought it by mistake, thinking it was a thriller, but decides to read it anyway; and Person four because she is the wife of the author and feels it is her duty to do so. These seem like fair enough reasons, but would it then be fair for you to say, "Yes, but what is the *one cause* for all of these people to read the book?" Must we assume that there is one cause over and above the causes for each individual?

Paul Edwards has presented an example to demonstrate Russell's criticism. Edwards asks us to imagine five Inuit who visit New York. A different explanation can be given as to why each Inuit is in New York: the first wanted warmer weather, the second is the husband of the first, the third is the son of the first and second, the fourth is responding to an advertisement in the New York Times asking for Inuit to appear on television, and the fifth has been hired by a private detective agency to keep an eye on the fourth. Although an individual explanation can be given why each Inuit is in New York, it does not make sense to then ask the one reason why the group as a whole are in New York.

3.2 David Hume

Russell's second argument above is also present in an important work by the Scottish philosopher **David Hume** (1711-76). In his *Dialogues Concerning Natural Religion* he states:

> "…the whole, you say, wants a cause. I answer, that the uniting of these parts into a whole, like the uniting of several distinct counties into one kingdom, or several distinct members into one body, is performed merely by an arbitrary act of the mind, and has no influence on the nature of things." (David Hume, *Dialogues Concerning Natural Religion*)

Hume will be referred to throughout this book as a critic of many of the arguments for the existence of God, and he is a recommended read. Hume believed that neither logic nor experience compel us to accept that everything must have a cause. What we observe is events in a sequence, and it is our minds that impose on this sequence the idea of causation or 'necessary connection'. This means that we cannot argue that there is any necessity to the notion that every event must have a cause, which means it cannot be used as a secure basis for an argument about the origins of the universe.

Hume argues that it is ridiculous to continue to trace causes beyond that which our experience provides evidence for, and that we might as well stop at the material world as anywhere else.

3.3 Other criticisms

There are a number of other philosophers that have a say in the debate: too many to do justice to in this chapter. For example, another great British philosopher, **John Stuart Mill** (1806-1873), in his article *Theism*, said: "Our experience, instead of furnishing an argument for a first cause, is repugnant to it." Likewise, the German philosopher **Immanuel Kant** (1724-1804), in his *Critique of Pure Reason*, says that the causal principle "is applicable only in the sensible world [the world we can experience with our senses]; outside that world it has no meaning whatsoever." Kant believed we have, if you like, our own 'human spectacles' that make us see the world in a certain way; though not necessarily the world as it really is. To talk of the cause of the universe is quite simply beyond our perception, and so it makes no sense to try to explain it or, for that matter, attempt to prove God's existence.

A modern philosopher who will often be referred to in this book is **Richard Swinburne** (1934-). Swinburne, who is a professor of the philosophy of religion at Oxford University, has attempted to bring many of the arguments for the existence of God into more modern discourse. When considering the cause of the universe, Swinburne would appeal to the principle of **Ockham's Razor** which, basically, states that, all other things being equal, one should prefer the simplest explanation over more complex ones. In other words, why complicate things with multiple explanations when a simple one suffices? For Swinburne, "God is simpler than anything we can imagine and gives a simple explanation for the system." However, someone like Bertrand Russell might well retort that stating that the universe 'just is' is as simple as you can get!

Perhaps the most immediate criticism that comes to mind is, 'Who caused God?' since an essential aspect of the argument is the insistence that everything must have a cause. But if one accepts that, it seems a little illogical to say that God cannot be included in this 'everything'. However, the point that supporters of the cosmological argument are making is that God is *not* part of 'everything' in the sense of all things in the universe because God exists *outside* the universe. God, to be God, is above and beyond causal laws.

Much of the cosmological argument rests upon the difficulties of the concept of infinity. Many are inclined towards the notion that all things, including the universe, must have a beginning. Many scientists argue for a 'Big Bang'. Again, a number of scientists accept the possibility that there are a series of 'Big Bangs', but then we are confronted with the difficulties of infinity. Consequently, either we accept that there is no beginning, or – in the case of Bertrand Russell for example – it is pointless attempting to give an explanation for the universe: it is 'just there'. This, however, hardly seems like a scientific explanation. As the theologian Keith Ward states in *God, Chance and Necessity*: "To say that such a very complex and well-ordered universe comes into being without any cause or reason is equivalent to throwing one's hands up in the air and just saying that anything at all might happen, that it is hardly worth bothering to look for reasons at all. And that is the death of science."

However, a retort to this might be that science deals with the world *as it is*, not in fantasies. For example, in addressing the question of origins it is straightforward to answer the question, 'What is the origin of my table?' In answering this question, you can detail the building process, the raw materials that make it up, and so on. In fact, the same question can be asked as to the origin of the earth, so long as it is answered in the context of the raw material that make it up. However, to then ask what is the origin of the whole universe is to enter a totally different realm: we are no longer dealing with the raw material but 'something outside'. It is not that the scientist *can't* answer the question, but that there *isn't* an answer to the question. That is, there is no raw material 'outside' the universe, therefore there is no answer and, in fact, the question itself does not make sense. It is rather like asking, 'how many sides does a circle have?' or 'why do humans grow wings?' The response to this is there isn't an answer.

Theologians such as Aquinas and Coppleston have attempted to show that there must be a necessary being, and that this is the best explanation available, whereas Swinburne argues that the theistic explanation is, *at the very least*, as good as the atheistic explanation. Either we are confronted with the conclusion that there is no explanation, that we have yet to find an explanation, or that we must accept the best explanation. Even though the cosmological argument does not demonstrate the existence of the Biblical God (and, perhaps, this is not its intention) it does raise the issue of whether or not there is an underlying reality to the universe and, in fact, whether it is justifiable to even consider such a possibility.

Further reading

Aquinas, T, *Summa Theologica*, Eyre & Spottiswoode, 1964.

Craig, W, *The Cosmological Argument from Plato to Leibniz*, MacMillan, 1980.

Davis, Stephen, *God, Reason and Theistic Proofs*, Edinburgh University Press, 1997. (Chaps. 4 & 8)

Davies, Brian, *An Introduction to the Philosophy of Religion*, OUP, 1993. (Chap. 5)

Hume, David, *Dialogues Concerning Natural Religion*, Penguin, 1990

Le Poidevin, Robin, *Arguing for Atheism*, Routledge, 1996. (Chap.1)

Quinn, Philip L. and Charles Taliaferro, *A Companion to Philosophy of Religion*, Blackwell, 1999. (Chap. 42)

Russell, Bertrand, *Why I Am Not a Christian*, Routledge, 1992.

Stump, Eleanor & Michael J. Murray (ed), *Philosophy of Religion: The Big Questions*, Blackwell, 1999. (Chap. 11)

Thompson, Mel, *Teach Yourself Philosophy of Religion*, Hodder & Stoughton, 1997. (Chap.4)
Vardy, Peter, *The Puzzle of God*, Fount, 1999 edition. (Chap. 7)

Chapter Three
THE TELEOLOGICAL ARGUMENT

'What could be more clear or obvious when we look up to the sky and contemplate the heavens, than that there is some divinity of superior intelligence?'

(Cicero, *On the Nature of the Gods*)

People have never failed to be awed by the seeming order of creation. For the Roman writer, poet and philosopher **Cicero** (106-43 BCE), the wonder of the heavens was enough to convince him that there must be some kind of superior intelligence to explain the order and beauty that was presented before him. In a similar vein, **Xenophon** in the fourth century BCE, quotes Socrates as saying, "With such signs of forethought in the design of living creatures, can you doubt they are the work of choice or design?"

This is where the teleological argument (also known as the '**design argument'**) begins. When we look at our world and, even further, beyond our world to the stars in the heavens, we cannot help but be astounded by its order and beauty, and so we are led to conclude that such intricate complexity must be designed in some way – it cannot occur of its own accord. The word 'teleological' comes from the Greek *'telos'* meaning 'purpose' or 'aim', and so it suggests that nature has been designed with some goal in mind. It was typical of the ancient Greeks to believe that there must *be* a purpose, of course, which, as we shall see, is a very different attitude to that of many contemporary thinkers who see the universe as purposeless. Consequently, how you perceive the world we live in will ultimately colour your view of the teleological argument.

1. THE MECHANICAL UNIVERSE
1.1 An argument from analogy

When we look at the history of the teleological argument we can find references that go back much further than the Christian tradition. In its broadest sense it is an argument to support the thesis that the universe is designed, not necessarily that it is the creation of a theistic God. When the Greeks spoke of a cosmic designer they obviously had no idea of the God conceived by the Jewish, Christian and Muslim traditions. Speculations on the notion of the universe as designed have a long history. Plato also presented an early version of the teleological argument, which can be found in his *Laws* (Book X).

Thomas Aquinas' 'Fifth Way' is also a version. Aquinas' Fifth Way has links with his first Three Ways, in his belief that the universe displays evidence of movement and cause and that things must move towards some specific end, "as an arrow is directed by the archer".

However, the theologian **William Paley** (1743-1805) together with the great critic of the teleological argument, David Hume, offer more modern and complex interpretations. Keep in mind that both Hume and Paley were writing at the time of the scientific revolution. The new scientific picture of the world that emerged in the Seventeenth Century, following the discoveries by scientists such as Kepler, Galileo and Newton, brought into question a number of religious claims. First, science demanded that theories should be tested. Second, the universe was perceived in a mechanical way: Newton saw the motion of the planets, and all motion, to be subject to the same laws of mechanics.

As astronomers perceived the universe as a very large mechanism, William Paley, in his book *Natural Theology* (1803), compares the world to a machine, with God as the great machine maker. He asks us to imagine he is walking across a heath and kicks a stone. He assumes that the stone has always been there and there is nothing remarkable about that. However, if he was then to come across a watch the same thing cannot be assumed. When the watch is inspected it is shown to have been put together for a specific purpose and that it contains order and regulation. Why can't the same assumption be made for the stone?

If you were to inspect the watch more carefully you would note that it has many parts that work in an orderly, regular and precise manner. Assuming you have never seen a watch before you would still infer that the watch has a purpose of some kind and that it must, therefore, have had a maker. What Paley is doing here is using the **argument from an effect to its cause**: you look at the effect (the watch), and then determine what caused it (the watchmaker). But what has this got to do with the universe? Paley makes the link by using an **argument from analogy**. Paley notes that nature – like a watch – is orderly, regular and precise and, therefore, concludes that nature is a complex machine. If we are to infer that the watch has a watchmaker, then we must also conclude that the universe has a divine maker.

Paley also uses the example of the eye to demonstrate how its various parts co-operate to produce sight. In the same way the eye has a specific purpose, so does the wings of a bird, or the fins of a fish.

Not only is there *purpose* in the world, but *regularity*: drawing on evidence from astronomy and Newton's laws of motion and gravity, Paley aimed to prove that there is design in the universe, for example, in the rotation of the planets in the solar system and how they hold their orbits and obey universal laws. Paley believed this could not have occurred merely by chance:

> "While the possible laws of variations were infinite, the admissible laws, or the compatible laws compatible with the system, lie within narrow limits. If the attracting forces had varied according to any direct law of the distance, let it have been what it would, great destruction and confusion would have taken place." (William Paley, *Natural Theology*)

Paley's argument can be summarised like this:

1. The universe is orderly
2. Order is the result of design
3. Design presupposes intelligence
4. As the universe is also complex in design, there must be a complex intelligence which designed it.
5. Therefore, this superior intelligence is God

1.2 A brief lesson in logic

The teleological argument, as already said, is an argument from analogy. Ultimately, the main question that needs to be addressed in this chapter is whether or not it is a *good* analogy and, if not, what better explanation for the apparent order in the universe can be given. If it can be argued that the teleological argument is the best explanation possible, then it is a strong argument.

To understand the process, it helps to have a brief lesson in basic logic, simply because the argument presented has a logical structure. A very common form of logic used in philosophy is the **syllogism**. For example:

All philosophers are wise
Socrates is a philosopher
Therefore, Socrates is wise

Or

All cats have four legs
Max is a cat
Therefore, Max has four legs

What you will, hopefully, notice about the above two examples is that they follow the basic format of:

All Ps are Qs (Premise 1)
S is a P (Premise 2)
Therefore, S is a Q (Conclusion)

This basic syllogism is an example of **deductive logic**: it guarantees the truth of the conclusion *provided* the premises are true. In other words, although you have to observe the world to make sure the premises are true, you do not have to observe the world to reach the conclusion – it is evident by deduction. Provided you follow this structure, the argument is **deductively valid**, even if the conclusion itself may be false.

The ontological argument, which we will look at in the next chapter, is one example of a deductive argument. The teleological argument, however, is not deductive; it is **inductive.** It is not claiming that the conclusion *must* be true, only that it is the *most consistent, most reasonable explanation.* Even if all the premises are correct, this does not guarantee that the conclusion is true, only that it is the best conclusion available. So, ask yourself this: is Paley's explanation the best available for the apparent order in the universe?

1.3 Hume's attack

Remember that one consequence of the scientific revolution was the requirement that knowledge should be *testable* if it is to be given any credence. For example, if you were to say that a stone sinks when you throw it in the water, then throwing a stone in the water can test this claim. The more stones you throw in the water, provided they do all sink each time, then the stronger the claim has to be credible. This form of acquiring knowledge is known as **empiricism**: the reliance upon observation and experience of the world in order to obtain knowledge of it. Of course, the difficulty with many religious claims is that they are not so readily subject to empirical testing: when someone says 'God exists' the empiricist cannot take out his tools of observation and test the claim in the same way he can test whether the planet Mars exists.

Before Paley, David Hume wrote his *Dialogues Concerning Natural Religion* (written in the 1750s). Hume was an empiricist, as well as an atheist. Atheism was still quite a dangerous thing to publicise at that time and, as a precaution, his *Dialogues* was not published until after his death at his request. 'Natural religion' is a reference to the belief that religious knowledge could be attained by inference from facts about the natural world. This is to be contrasted with 'revealed religion', which argues that religious knowledge comes from revelation. As an empiricist, Hume was keen to show that a study of the natural world could not succeed in telling us anything about the Christian concept of God.

In this book, a conversation takes place between three philosophers, Demea, Cleanthes, and Philo. Cleanthes represents the supporter of the teleological argument, describing the world as a great machine sub-divided into lesser machines. A study of the world shows that its order and arrangement resembles the results of human contrivance. We are, therefore, led to infer that "the Author of nature is somewhat similar to the mind of man", though far superior in intelligence to that of man. The character of Philo then proceeds to demolish the argument. We can probably safely assume that the arguments of Philo are those of Hume.

Hume's *Dialogues* is an entertaining and enlightening read and is highly recommended. What you will see is that Hume is attacking Paley's premises (although written before Paley), and thus seemingly weakening the whole argument.

Although Hume's arguments overlap somewhat, and it is difficult to classify them separately, I believe he does address each of Paley's premises in the following manner:

First Premise: The universe is orderly

"Look round the universe. What an immense profusion of beings, animated and organised, sensible and active! ... The whole presents nothing but the idea of a blind nature, impregnated by a great vivifying principle, and pouring forth from her lap, without discernment or parental care, her maimed and abortive children!" (David Hume, *Dialogues Concerning Natural Religion*)

Paley's argument would not be a problem if it were morally neutral. When we talk of the design of a watch, morality does not come into it: the watchmaker does not need to be morally good to make a good watch. However, the world is an entirely different matter if we are trying to conclude that it is made by a good (morally good) designer, for the world evidently is not morally good. When we look at the world it does not appear to be as happy, ordered and harmonious as one might wish. There is seemingly arbitrary mass destruction, disease, creatures torturing and killing other creatures, pain and illness. Why would a benevolent God let such things happen? Or why would an omnipotent God create a world where such things *have* to happen? Some would consider this the principle argument against a designer, leastwise a *benevolent* designer. The notion of the universe as a beautiful, orderly place seems to lack much credence in the face of harsh, cruel reality. (This is also an argument related to the problem of evil, which is examined in Chapter Ten.)

Over the past thirty years or so it has become clearer that the motion of many physical systems (including planets) are not as regular as Newton had suggested. In other words, nature appears not to be as mechanical as the machines we make, and, therefore, the analogy does not work. Such a theory seems to lend support to Hume's thesis that there is no obvious sense in which the universe is orderly in the way that human production is. In fact, it could be argued that human production is 'better' than the universe, which is why we feel the need to produce things in the first place.

Second Premise: Order is the result of design

"If we see a house...we conclude, with the greatest certainty, that it had an architect or builder, because this is precisely that species of effect, which we have experienced to proceed from that species of cause. But surely you will not affirm, that the universe bears such a resemblance to a house, that we can with the same certainty infer a similar cause, or that the analogy is here entire and perfect." (David Hume, *Dialogues Concerning Natural Religion*)

For Paley, if it can be shown that something has order then there must be someone who creates that order. This, as was mentioned earlier, is the argument from effect to cause: the effect being the order that is witnessed, the cause being that which creates the order. If one adopts the empiricist approach, our knowledge of causes and effects is based on our experience. For example, you know that if you cut yourself with a knife then you will bleed and feel pain. But *how* do your know this? Either because you have experienced it before, you've seen it happen to someone else, or you have been told by an authority that you trust that this is what happens. Now, following from this, you know that when you see a house it had a builder and an architect. How? Again, not because you were born with this knowledge or that it just 'came to you'. You know by experience. You have seen many houses being built. But can you say the same about the universe? Have you witnessed a universe being built? In this way, the universe is unique as we have not experienced its creation.

Third Premise: Design presupposes intelligence

"If we survey a ship, what an exalted idea must we form of the ingenuity of the carpenter, who framed so complicated useful and beautiful machine? And what surprise must we entertain, when we find him a stupid mechanic, who imitated others, and copied an art, which, through a long succession of ages, after multiplied trials, mistakes, corrections, deliberations, and controversies, had been gradually improving?" (David Hume, *Dialogues Concerning Natural Religion*)

Consider the analogy of a ship and its builders. You can admire the beauty and complexity of, say, an ocean liner, but this was made by a large number of people; why not the same with the world? It could be made by a number of 'lesser deities' or even demons! Of course, this still does point to the fact that there is a designer and that the designer, or designers, have an intelligence of some kind or other, but the point Hume is making that it does not in itself point to the classical definition of the *Christian God*, who is a single entity and the supreme intelligence.

Fourth Premise: As the universe is so complex in design, there must be a complex intelligence

"This world, for aught he knows, is very faulty and imperfect, compared to a superior standard; and was only the first rude essay of some infant deity; who afterwards abandoned it, ashamed of his lame performance: It is the work only of some dependent, inferior deity; and is the object of derision to his superiors." (David Hume, *Dialogues Concerning Natural Religion*)

How can we be sure that this universe is so complex? This universe, if it is made by a creator, could actually be something of a 'botched job' compared to other universes! However complex it may seem to us, we only have this universe to base our judgements on. As we cannot compare the workings of this universe with any other, then we cannot conclude that this universe is a particularly complex one. For example, a person who has never encountered machinery of any kind would consider a slide rule complex, but compared to modern-day computers, it is actually very simple.

Taking the criticisms of all four premises into account, how can we then conclude that there is a superior intelligence at all and that this intelligence must be God? Hume's argument that there is nothing else like the universe is a strong one. The teleological argument might well be a convincing argument if we have had experience of hundreds of universes being built, but we have not, so how can we make such an inference that the universe, by analogy, is designed?

2. ATTACK REBUFFED? THE MODERN DEBATE
2.1 Swinburne's response

Remember, we are trying to find the best explanation possible and, by 'best', we mean an argument that is simple, clear, rational and coherent. What we need to do is to see the extent to which Hume has shown the teleological argument to be a poor one, and whether or not Hume is able to present a better explanation for the nature of the universe. In fact, current versions of the teleological argument proceed not in terms of analogies between the universe and human creations, but as arguments to the best explanation based upon data from our experience. For this we need to bring the debate up to date with the philosopher Richard Swinburne.

First premise revisited

You will recall that the very first premise concentrates on the universe as having order. This, of course, is the central premise of the whole argument. Hume argued that the universe is not as ordered and harmonious as supposed and so there is no need to suggest a designer. Swinburne, however, presented Paley's argument in a more modern, concise manner. He argued that there are two kinds of order: **spatial order** (what he calls 'regularities of copresence') and **temporal order** ('regularities of succession').

Spatial order is observed at *one instant in time*. This is like taking a snapshot with a still camera of one moment. For example, you open the bonnet of a stationary car and see the parts of an engine without seeing these parts in motion over a period of time. You can observe how each part fits with other parts but you are not aware of how this structure will develop and change when in use. Temporal order, however, is concerned with *a period of time*. For example, patterns of behaviour (laws of nature, cause and effect) or the movement of the car from A to B. Now, of course, order in nature can have both spatial and temporal dimensions but Paley concentrated on spatial order only, which, argues Swinburne, puts him on "slippery ground".

Swinburne readily admits that if you examine the universe at *one instant in time* then there is a great deal of disorder. Take, for example, the African jungle. It appears to be a veritable mess, with trees of all different shapes and sizes, inefficient flora and fauna, and so on. However, to take that view would be to ignore the bigger picture. According to Swinburne, over *a period of time* we see that the jungle has a finely tuned eco-system that is able to adapt to changing circumstances and conditions and *appears to be* purposeful. Swinburne readily credits Aquinas with the importance of temporal order. His Fifth Way states: "An ordinance of actions to an end is observed in all bodies obeying natural laws, even when they lack awareness." However, Swinburne's view of nature as possessing the ability to adapt in some meaningful way is not always backed up by the evidence: whole ecosystems can fail to adapt and can seem to the non-theistic observer as totally inefficient.

Second premise revisited

What of Hume's attack of the second premise, that we have not experienced the creation of the universe and so we cannot conclude that it has a designer? Swinburne's retort to this is that much of science is also based upon weak conclusions that bear no relation to experience. Before mankind had even gone so far as the Moon, scientists were concluding that the origins of the universe lay in a cosmic 'Big Bang'. This is by inference from what can be observed in the present time. It is observing the laws of microphysics and extrapolating back to the first few seconds of cosmic history. However, no one has actually *experienced* the Big Bang.

Remember that we are looking for *the best possible explanation*. The teleological argument is an argument for the existence of God, not *concrete proof* that God exists. As a consequence, we have to ask whether or not it is a good argument compared with any other. As we have not experienced the creation of the universe we either must adopt the best possible explanation, or conclude that there can be no explanation.

Third premise revisited

Why should we suppose, as Paley's third premise does, that the beginning of the universe rests with an intelligent designer? Swinburne argues that as rational agents (i.e. human beings) produce many ordered things that exist in our world then, by analogy, the order that the universe possesses points to a rational agent as the best explanation. As the universe is so complex, this suggests a complex rational agent. Further, in order to create something, the creator cannot be part of the creation, and so the creator would have to exist outside of the universe. Here, Swinburne is arguing for a "very powerful free non-embodied rational agent." This he admits, is not quite the same as arguing for the Biblical God; but at least it's a start!

However, what of Hume's criticism that the universe could have been designed by many rational agents? In fact, these agents could, in Hume's words, be "stupid mechanics". However, Swinburne has pointed out that Hume himself has said, "To multiply causes, without necessity, is indeed contrary to true philosophy." You may recall from the previous chapter that this reflects the principle of Ockham's Razor. Therefore, why suggest many gods when the one God will do?

Fourth premise revisited

Hume's criticism of the fourth premise is that we cannot be sure that the universe is really that complex or well-ordered at all, as we have nothing to compare it to. Richard Swinburne has pointed out that part of this criticism rests upon the thesis that we need many universes to compare this universe with to show that this universe is a well-designed one. It is rather like possessing a car that seems to run quite smoothly, gets you from A to B without breaking down and, basically, does the job it is supposed to do, but refusing to accept that your car is well-designed until you compare it with many other cars. For Swinburne, using the principle of Ockham's Razor once more, this is just another example of explaining the presence of our universe by appealing to many universes created by many gods, rather than adopting the simpler approach of one universe created by one God.

Even if it is suggested that we may not perceive the universe as ordered as *we* might like it to be, that is not to deny that there *is* order and, amongst many scientists, there is a perception of a pattern in the universe. One probably needs to be a mathematician to really appreciate the beauty that is maths, or a physicist to appreciate the wonder of physical laws. Yet those of us who are not scientists can appreciate beautiful music, art or poetry. As music, art and poetry are designed by an intelligence, is there some justification for assuming the same is true for physical laws?

3. CHALLENGES OF SCIENCE
3.1 The selfish gene

In 1831, a young British scientist by the name of **Charles Darwin** (1809-1882), sailed to the coast of South America on the survey ship HMS Beagle. He went to study the flora and fauna of the islands in that region, most famously the curious animal life on the Galapagos Islands. One of the puzzles at that time was why the planet was not more heavily populated with life than it actually was. Considering the extent to which animals breed, the planet would be bulging at the seams with animal life even if history was only measured in biblical years (which, incidentally, was calculated in the seventeenth century by Archbishop James Ussher from the lineages in the Bible that Creation took place in 4004 BCE...in October!). The most popular theory was the **catastrophe theory**, which proposed that the world had experienced a series of catastrophes of some kind. One version of this theory stated that the most recent catastrophe was the event recorded in the Bible as the Great Flood when Noah took the male and female of each species into his Ark. The important point of this theory is that the animals that God created at the beginning of time have not changed in any way since then.

Darwin, however, noted that on each island he travelled to the animals of the same species (for example, the remarkable giant tortoises that he encountered) differed from those on other islands in terms of eating habits and so on. He concluded that these creatures, though possessing a common ancestry, had evolved differently according to their different environments. This he considered far more credible a theory than God creating at one moment in time all these animals slightly different from each other.

In 1859, Charles Darwin published *The Origin of the Species,* which concluded that species evolve from other species, and that natural selection is the principal mechanism that produces these changes. The main relevance of this theory for the teleological argument is that new species could be formed without the need for a God. Life evolves naturally; it was not created in the sense of Genesis; nor is God required to regulate the world.

An important 'neo-Darwinian' is **Richard Dawkins** (1941-), who stated in his readable book *The Blind Watchmaker,* "Although atheism might have been intellectually tenable before Darwin, Darwin made it possible to be an intellectually fulfilled atheist."

Charles Darwin is not questioning Paley's premise that there is order in the universe, only that there must be *purpose.* Richard Dawkins suggests that the 'Why?' question is not always appropriate. In *River Out of Eden* (1995) he says,

> "We find it hard to look at anything without wondering what it is 'for', what the motive for it is, or the purpose behind it. When the obsession with purpose becomes pathological it is called paranoia – reading malevolent purpose into what is actually random bad luck." (Richard Dawkins, *River Out of Eden*)

Dawkins provides the example of the cheetah and the antelope. If we attempt to establish purpose for their existence we would conclude that the cheetah's primary purpose (what he calls its **'utility function'**) is to kill antelopes. Do the same for antelopes, and its primary purpose is to run as fast as possible away from cheetahs and, in the process, causing the starvation of cheetahs. As he states:

> "...if there is only one Creator who made the tiger and the lamb, the cheetah and the gazelle, what is He playing at? Is He a sadist who enjoys spectator sports?" (Richard Dawkins, *River Out of Eden*)

The mistake, according to Dawkins, is that we assume that humans have a specific purpose, a particular, unique 'utility function' yet, in actual fact, there is only one single utility function of life, and that is DNA survival.

3.2 The anthropic principle

Even if we find the argument that we are the result of design unconvincing, or that the universe is not as ordered or harmonious as first supposed it still strikes many as puzzling, if not miraculous, that we exist in the first place. For example, if the conditions of life were different by the tiniest of fractions then life as we know it would not exist. An analogy with, say, a car's engine, can be used: if a certain part of the engine is out of sync then you end up with a rattling noise or a breakdown. However, if you 'fine-tune' the engine, then it runs smoothly. The same is true of the universe; it runs smoothly. To support carbon-based life-forms the universe has just the right amount of carbon, just the right amount of helium, just the right amount of radiation, and so on. In fact, the odds of this universe existing with intelligent, carbon-based life, are extremely low. This argument is what is known as the **anthropic principle**: if the fundamental principles had been only fractionally different, things could not have evolved in the way they have.

The anthropic principle is a relatively recent development in the teleological argument and was developed by **F.R. Tennant**, in his book *Philosophical Theology* (1930):

> "The forcibleness of Nature's suggestion that she is the outcome of intelligent design lies not in particular cases of adaptedness in the world, nor even in the multiplicity of them…it consists rather in the conspiration of innumerable causes to produce, by either united and reciprocal action, and to maintain, a general order of Nature." (F. R. Tennant, *Philosophical Theology*)

By the 'conspiration of innumerable causes', Tennant is arguing that there are just too many interlinked events and effects for them to be mere coincidence or the product of a chaotic universe. Accepting Darwin's evolutionary thesis, Tennant sees this as part of God's plan; the evolutionary process was designed to create an environment that would support intelligent life. Arthur Brown is another supporter of this principle:

> "The ozone gas layer is a mighty proof of the creator's forethought. Could anyone possibly attribute this device to a chance evolutionary process? A wall which prevents death to every living thing, just the right thickness and

exactly the correct defence gives every evidence of a plan."(Arthur Brown, *Footprints of God*)

However, a criticism of this is that the universe is as it is because we are in a position to observe it. In other words, we cannot possibly be surprised that the laws of nature are how they are, for if they were any different we would not be here to *be* surprised. Imagine a prisoner who is about to be executed in front of a firing squad of ten men. The men point the rifles at their target, fire, and all ten miss. The man who was to be executed is asked: "Don't you think it is a miracle that all ten missed?" He responds: "Of course not. If they hadn't missed then I wouldn't be here now." The prisoner may well have responded with, "Indeed this was a miracle, an act of God," but instead adopts the attitude that there is no reason to be surprised and that there is no explanation necessary. The question seems to come down to whether or not we should be surprised by seeming improbabilities.

Alongside the anthropic principle, Tennant also put forward the **aesthetic argument** for the existence of God. Tennant argued that there are certain qualities humans posses that cannot be explained by evolutionary theory, for example the ability to make and appreciate music, or great works of art. If such an ability is not necessary for the survival of the human species, then why do we possess them? Is not this ability to appreciate and create beauty evidence of a creator?

> "Nature is not just beautiful in places, it is saturated with beauty - on the telescopic and microscopic scale. Our scientific knowledge brings us no nearer to understanding the beauty of music." (F.R. Tennant, *Philosophical Theology*)

However, a response to this was made by the modern philosopher Daniel Dennett:

> "You think that natural selection can explain a nightingale but not 'An Ode To A Nightingale'? You think 'An Ode To A Nightingale' is that much more wonderful than the nightingale itself? What hubris!" (*Does God Exist?*, In-Tele-Com/Teleacc-Not/Swedich Educational Broadcasting, 1999)

Further reading

Cole, Peter, *Philosophy of Religion,* Hodder & Stoughton, 1999. (Chap. 4)

Davis, Stephen, *God, Reason and Theistic Proofs*, Edinburgh University Press, 1997. (Chap. 6)

Davies, Brian, *An Introduction to the Philosophy of Religion*, OUP, 1993. (Chap. 6)

Dawkins, Richard, *The Selfish Gene*, Oxford Paperbacks, 1989.

Dawkins, Richard, *The Blind Watchmaker*, Penguin, 1991.

Dawkins, Richard, *River Out of Eden: A Darwinian View of Life*, Weidenfield and Nicholson, 1995.

Hick, John, *Philosophy of Religion*, Prentice Hall, 1963. (Chap. 2)

Hume, David, *Dialogues Concerning Natural Religion*, Penguin, 1990.

Le Poidevin, Robin, *Arguing For Atheism*, Routledge, 1996. (Chaps. 4 & 5)

Paley, William, 'The Watch and the Watchmaker', in *The Existence of God* ed. by John Hick, Macmillan, 1964.

Quinn, Philip L. and Charles Taliaferro, *A Companion to Philosophy of Religion*, Blackwell, 1999. (Chap. 43)

Swinburne, Richard, 'The Argument from Design', from *Philosophy*, 43, 1968.

Tennant, F.R., 'Cosmic Teleology', in *The Existence of God,* ed. by John Hick, Macmillan, New York.

Thompson, Mel, *Teach Yourself Philosophy of Religion,* Hodder & Stoughton, 1997. (Chap.4)

Vardy, Peter, *The Puzzle of God,* Fount, 1999. (Chap. 9)

Ward, Keith, *God, Chance and Necessity*, Oneworld, 1996.

Chapter Four
THE ONTOLOGICAL ARGUMENT

"Why then did 'the Fool say in his heart, that there is no God' when it is so evident to any rational mind that You of all things exist to the highest degree? Why indeed, unless because he was stupid and a fool?"

(St. Anselm, *Proslogion*)

Can we prove that God exists simply by *thinking* of God? In other words, is it possible to prove that God must exist on the basis that you have an idea of God in your mind? According to the philosopher and theologian **St. Anselm** (1033-1109), it is indeed possible.

The ontological argument is different from the previous two arguments we have considered in that is an *a priori* argument. The cosmological argument and the teleological argument, you may recall, are *a posteriori*. *A posteriori* knowledge is the most common form of knowledge we possess. This form of knowledge is based on experience. That is to say, we acquire it through observation, looking up the information in a reliable reference book, past experience, and so on. Two examples are my knowledge that Hitler was appointed Chancellor in 1933, or my knowledge that sunflowers have yellow petals.

However, it may be argued that not all of our knowledge comes from experience alone. Take, for example, the fact that 2+2=4. Such mathematical formulations, some would argue, can be determined *prior to* experience; provided, of course, you are already familiar with the number system. Anselm presents the view that the same could be said for the existence of God. His existence does not require proof by appeal to experience because we know he exists already. That is, you are not required to appeal to the external world, or some form of empirical evidence, to prove God's existence. Because we understand the language in which we operate, it is sufficient merely to reflect upon what is meant when we use the word 'God'.

As well as the ontological argument being *a priori*, it is also considered stronger than the *a posteriori* arguments because it argues that the definition of God is **analytically true**.

An example of an analytic statement is 'All bachelors are un-married men'. The reason this is an analytic statement is because it does not provide us with any new information. It is a tautology (a statement which uses different words to say the same thing) because 'bachelors' and 'unmarried men' mean the same thing. Provided we understand what the word 'bachelors' means in the first place (i.e. that they are unmarried men), then – other than linguistic information – we have not been given any information that elaborates or develops what these bachelors are. In more technical terms, the subject (bachelors) and the predicate (un-married men) are synonymous (they mean the same thing). There are many other examples of analytic statements. 'All sisters are female', 'Your father's father is your grandfather', and so on. These sentences are, therefore, analytic truths, or analytic propo-sitions.

Further, because the predicate gives you no additional infor-mation you do not have to *verify* it; that is, you don't have to ask every bachelor in the world if he is unmarried. Therefore, an analytic statement is also considered *a priori* because the knowl-edge that bachelors are unmarried men is known *prior to* engaging in any kind of empirical research. The statement is also a **neces-sary truth**: a bachelor *must* be an unmarried man. In the same way, mathematical statements are necessary truths: two plus two *must* equal four.

Analytic statements, therefore, are necessarily true. They don't need to appeal to experience. Another way of identifying analytic statements is that their negations are self-contradictory. For ex-ample, you cannot say 'bachelors are *not* unmarried men'.

On the other hand, many statements we come across are claim-ing to tell us something, to give us additional information about the world. These are what are known as **synthetic statements.**

An example of a synthetic statement is "all bachelors are happy" How does this differ from the analytic statement 'all bachelors are unmarried men'? If you think of the word 'bachelors' then it is not necessarily true all bachelors are happy. Even if the state-ment is true, it is not *necessarily* true: it is not necessary that bach-elors *must* be happy to be bachelors. In more technical terms, the predicate and subject are not synonymous. Here the predicate ('happy') certainly expresses an additional quality to that of the subject ('bachelors'). Further, it is *a posteriori*; you will have to (or have had to at some stage in the past) do a little empirical work to verify whether the statement is true or not. Although synthetic statements are not necessarily true they are, at least, subject to verification. That is, it can be verified whether all bachelors are happy or not.

1. ST. ANSELM'S FIRST ARGUMENT

St Anselm was born in northern Italy, became Abbot of Bec in Normandy, and later, Archbishop of Canterbury. He wrote a series of meditations called the *Monologion* ('*Soliloquy*', 1077) in which he spoke of God and His attributes. Encouraged by the positive reception to this work he wrote the *Proslogion* ('*Discourse*', 1077), the second chapter of which presented the original statement of what in the 18th century became known as the ontological argument for the existence of God. Ontology is a branch of metaphysics which is concerned with existence itself. Hence, the argument centres on the idea of God's existence.

As Anselm is central to the history of the ontological argument – for it had a distinct origin that goes back to him (not the Greeks this time!) – this chapter will concentrate on what he said in Chapters II and III of the *Proslogion*, as well as responses to it. Although Anselm himself did not appear to make such a distinction, most of the arguments in *Proslogion* Chapter II are logically distinct – though very similar – from what is presented in Chapter III. It is, therefore, best to consider each argument separately.

1.1 The greatest conceivable being

'And so, O Lord, since You give understanding to faith, give me to understand – as far as You know it to be good for me – that You do exist, as we believe, and that You are what we believe You to be. Now we believe that You are a being than which nothing greater can be conceived.' (St. Anselm, *Proslogion*)

For Anselm, faith and reason are not in conflict with one another, but rather act in partnership. Reason is an important tool for understanding, acting like a torch to illuminate what is understood by the term 'God'. The important part of the above quote is what Anselm meant by 'that You are a being than which nothing greater can be conceived'. Two key words here need to be clearly defined.

First of all, what did he mean by 'conceived' (some translations use the word 'thought')? If you were to read the *Proslogion* as a whole, it appears that the primary meaning of 'conceived' is to be able to imagine that which is *logically possible*. That is to say, we can conceive of a being that is all-powerful, all-knowing and so on, but this is not the same as a being that can square circles or create a being greater than himself, which is logically impossible

When Anselm talks of God as 'a being than which nothing greater can be conceived', we need to determine what he means by 'great'. Although Anselm himself does not define what he meant by this, it seems apparent from his writings that he is not merely limiting himself to 'goodness', but is using it in a more all-encompassing manner. 'Great' covers a range of positive attributes, such as all-powerful, all-knowing and so on. It is obvious that he did not mean the greatest being that you or I can possibly think (or conceive) of, simply because we are limited in our conceptions. The very fact that Anselm meditates upon the property of God as being 'the greatest being' means that God must be greater than the human conception of 'greatness'. We can, for example, imagine – or conceive of – something or someone that is 'powerful'. We may associate the term with an historical figure – Napoleon, for example – or an imaginary figure, such as Superman. We would say that Superman is more powerful than Napoleon, and we may even be able to conceive of a person even more powerful than Superman; but our conceptions are still limited in relation to the power that God possesses.

Having at least some idea of what Anselm meant by his terms, lets look at the main points of the argument in Chapter II, which can be set out in four steps. It may, at first, seem quite complicated, but if you read through the four points below a few times you should see that it is quite a logical approach. What you need to do is think to yourself: what, if anything, is *wrong* with this logic?

We all can conceive of things in the mind that we deny exist in reality

"...Or is there no such nature, since the fool hath said in his heart, there is no God? (Psalms xiv.1). But, at any rate, this very fool, when he hears of this being of which I speak – a being than which nothing greater can be conceived – understands what he hears, and what he understands is in his understanding; although he does not understand it to exist..." (St. Anselm, *Proslogion*)

The 'fool' in this case is the atheist who, in Psalms 14 of the Bible, denied that God exists. Anselm argued that in order to deny the existence of something you must have some conception of what it is you are denying. I can say 'Superman does not exist' but only if I have some idea of who Superman is. In other words, communication between the believer and non-believer is possible. Although both dispute God's existence, both readily make use of the term 'God'. In this respect, the non-believer has some conception of a God as an omnipotent being; the only difference is that he denies the actual existence of such a God. Anselm here is also arguing that the statement 'God is that than which nothing greater can be conceived' is an *analytic statement*: provided you understand the term 'God' then it must follow that its meaning is the greatest being; to state otherwise is a self-contradiction (you cannot say 'God is *not* the greatest being that can be conceived')

That which exists in the mind could exist in reality

"And assuredly that, than which nothing greater can be conceived, cannot exist in the understanding alone. For, suppose it exists in the understanding alone; then it can be conceived to exist in reality." (St. Anselm, *Proslogion*)

At the moment, Anselm is only suggesting that if you can conceive of something in the mind, then there is at least the *possibility* it might exist in reality. I can, for example, conceive in my mind of a man who flies through the air, wearing his underpants outside his trousers, and possessing special powers. This is not the same, of course, as saying my conception *does* exist in reality.

Things that exist in reality must be greater than things that exist only in the mind

"If that, than which nothing greater can be conceived, exists in the understanding alone, the very being, than which nothing greater can be conceived is one, than which a greater can be conceived. But obviously this is impossible." (St. Anselm, *Proslogion*)

This is a vital point in the argument. Anselm suggests that if you can conceive of something greater in the mind and that there is a *possibility* that it exists, then its existence would be greater (in terms of more powerful, abler, freer, and so on) than a figment of someone's imagination. For example, you can conceive in your mind a fifty-pound note; how much greater this would be if it were a fifty-pound note in your pocket! If we accept the definition that God is 'a being than which nothing greater can be conceived,' and we also accept the argument that a being that exists in reality is considerably greater (more powerful) than one that exists in the mind, then God must exist. God in reality is far greater than God in the mind. Therefore:

God exists both in reality and in the mind.

> "Hence there is no doubt that there exists a being, than which nothing greater can be conceived, and it exists both in the understanding and in reality." (St. Anselm, *Proslogion*)

Provided we accept the possibility of 'the greatest being', and that which exists in reality is greater than that which exists in the mind, then God, as the greatest being, cannot exist only in the mind.

2. ST. ANSELM'S SECOND ARGUMENT
2.1 Gaunilo

The Benedictine monk Gaunilo of Marmoutier, a contemporary of Anselm, wrote a response to *Proslogion* called *On Behalf of the Fool*. Gaunilo, along with a number of other theologians, took offence at the idea that mere mortals could come any way at all to conceiving of God; we cannot come close to any understanding of His nature. Anselm would agree with Gaunilo that it is not possible for a mere human being to understand God in the same way as, say, we can understand basic mathematics – God is just too *different* for that. Nonetheless, he believes it is sufficient simply to understand the definition of God as 'a being than which nothing greater can be conceived' to grasp the *essence* of God.

However, Gaunilo's most famous criticism goes like this:

1. We can conceive of a perfect island
2. A perfect island must be more perfect in reality than in the mind
3. Therefore, a perfect island exists.

You can see that if you replace the phrase 'perfect island' with 'perfect being' (i.e. God) you effectively have Anselm's argument. According to Gaunilo, Anselm's logic must, therefore, be **fallacious** (i.e. there is a mistake in the logic) because you can use the same logical structure to prove the existence of all manner of things, such as a perfect island.

2.2 Anselm's retort

Anselm replied to this in his short work, *Reply to Gaunilo*. There is a serious fault with Gaunilo's use of an island or any other object for that matter. An island cannot be defined as 'that than which no greater island can be conceived' because you can always better an island (add some more sand, a few more palm trees, etc.), whereas, by definition, God cannot be bettered. In the phrase of the modern philosopher **Alvin Plantinga**, islands do not have an **'intrinsic maximum'**. Further, an island is *contingent* whereas God is not.

Anselm basically asked Gaunilo to refer to Chapter III of his *Proslogion*. In other words, Anselm claims to have already pre-empted Gaunilo's criticism. To understand this response, it is important to be reminded of two important concepts that were referred to in the previous chapter:

Contingent existence. A contingent thing (or being) is something (or someone) that logically might not have been. They are things that happen (the Latin for 'to happen' is *'contingere'*) to take place, but, if circumstances had been different, need not have taken place.

Necessary existence. The opposite of contingent. That is, they could not be other than what they are, *even if* circumstances had been different. If my parents had never met, I would not exist, *but* two plus two would still equal four.

Anselm went on to argue the following:

1. Either God exists or He does not exist.
2. If God exists, God's existence must be necessary.
3. If God does not exist, then his existence is logically impossible.
4. God is not a logically impossible thing.
5. Therefore, God's existence is necessary.
6. Therefore, God exists.

Let's go through each of these carefully:

Either God exists or He does not exist. There seems nothing to dispute here. Anselm is starting off on solid ground with a black or white statement.

If God exists, God's existence must be necessary. The emphasis here is on the 'if' word. Anselm is not asking you to believe in a necessary being, only that *if* God exists he must, by definition, be necessary.

If God does not exist, then his existence is logically impossible. We can talk of two types of things that exist: contingent things and necessary things. But what kinds of things can *not* exist? Again, there are two kinds: contingent things and logically impossible things.

Examples of contingent beings that do not exist (at least, so far as we know), are Superman, or unicorns, or Queen Victoria (she used to exist, but doesn't anymore). Examples of logically impossible things are square circles, male sisters, and so on. What of God? He is obviously not a contingent being because if He did exist, then He would be dependent upon His existence on something else, which, for God, is a contradiction. Therefore, if we are saying that God does not exist, then it must be because God is logically impossible.

God is not a logically impossible thing. The existence of God displays no logical contradiction and, therefore, it is logically possible for God to exist

Therefore, God's existence is necessary and *therefore, God exists.* As God is not logically impossible and also is not a contingent non-existent thing, then there is only one possible state left: that of a necessary being. It, therefore, follows that God's existence is necessary and God does exist.

If you read through the above a few times you will, hopefully, see that Anselm is being very clever here. If we accept that there might be a necessary being, then, by a process of elimination, God cannot be any other kind of being: He cannot be an existing contingent being (like you or me), or a non-existent contingent being (like the unicorn), or a logically impossible being (like an all-powerful God that is not all-powerful), or a necessary non-existent being (which is logically impossible). Therefore, God must be a necessary existent being.

The most important difference between this version of the argument and Anselm's first version is that it is not dependent upon existence as being a perfection or a matter of greatness. Rather than saying that God must exist because existence is a perfection, Anselm is saying that God must exist because He is a *necessary being.*

Interestingly, another theologian who agreed with Gaunilo that it is wrong to attempt to conceive of God's attributes was Aquinas, yet he then provides a definition of God as a necessary being in his Third Way. In fact, Aquinas' Third Way can be seen as also part of the ontological argument, in the same way as Coplestone's response to Russell.

3. MODERN SUPPORTERS AND CRITICS
3.1 René Descartes

A modern supporter of the ontological argument is the French philosopher **René Descartes** (1596-1650). Descartes is generally considered the inaugurator of modern philosophy, a great innovator who challenged conventional beliefs that were still to a very large extent based on Church authority.

Many regard Descartes' version of the ontological argument as more succinct and accessible for the modern-day reader. You would certainly gain by reading some of his book *Meditations* (1641). In this work, Descartes imagines the entire universe, even the apparent *a priori* truths of mathematics and geometry, to be the work of an 'evil demon' who is creating an illusion that such things exist.

This is what is famously known as the process of **Cartesian Doubt**; to 'bracket' all that we call knowledge and to start again from the foundations. In other words, what can we really *know* for sure? What is it that even an evil demon could not deceive us about? He begins with the one thing that is necessarily true: 'I am thinking, therefore I exist' (in Latin, **'cogito ergo sum'**). The *cogito*, as it is usually known, was first proclaimed in an earlier work, the *Discourse on Method* (1637), but it is in the *Meditations* that Descartes pushes the boundaries of the *Cogito* forward. This work was written in Latin because Descartes deliberately wanted it to be read by theologians (who still used Latin as their primary language of communication) and aimed to show that philosophy was no longer tied to the restrictions of scholasticism.

Having concluded that he can know that he exists (the existence of others is quite another matter), Descartes then considers what else is 'clear and distinct' in his mind. These include such *a priori* things as geometrical objects and numbers.

Descartes conceived of God as the perfect being and, as existence is more perfect than non-existence, then He exists. Existence is God's *essence* in the same way the essence of a mountain has both an uphill and a downhill slope (which, Descartes states, is what he meant by 'valley') or, to use another of Descartes' examples, the essence of a triangle is a 'three-sided plane figure'. The same, Descartes argues, applies when we think of God. We only have to think of God to associate Him with existence. Therefore to say, 'God does not exist' is rather like saying, 'A triangle does not have three sides'.

Whereas Anselm had Gaunilo to respond to, Descartes had the priest Caterus. Caterus argued that the statement '*If* God exists then he is the highest being' is, indeed, a tautology (that is, a repetition of the same word by using a different word); but he emphasises the *if*. It is not illogical or contradictory to say, 'God does not exist, therefore there is no highest being'. Likewise, we can say '*If* a triangle exists it has three sides', but we can also coherently say, 'triangles do not exist, therefore three sided things do not exist.'

3.2 Immanuel Kant

Certainly one of the greatest thinkers of modern times is the German philosopher **Immanuel Kant** (1724-1804). It is very difficult to summarise Kant's criticism without a wider under-standing of his whole philosophy, for he was one of the last great 'system-builders' and it is difficult to step into any aspect of his philosophy without it presupposing other aspects. Nonetheless, his is a very important criticism of Anselm and Descartes that has a large number of supporters. Also, it should be pointed out that Kant himself did believe in the existence of God, although he considered it pointless to attempt to *prove* God's existence.

Kant re-iterates the criticism by Caterus that there is no contra-diction in saying that if you dismiss the idea of a triangle and the idea of three sides, then you don't have a contradiction. Like-wise, if you dismiss the idea of God and the idea of God's exist-ence you also have no contradiction.

Kant raised a second objection that using the term 'exists' as if it has some real value is a mistake: the word 'exists' is not a *real predicate*. Kant made a distinction between a **logical predicate** and a **real predicate**. A logical predicate is any word that is placed in the predicate position of a sentence (that is, after the subject). For example:

The car [subject] is fast [predicate]

For Kant, anything at all can be a logical predicate. But this does not make it a *real predicate*. Using Kant's own terms, a real predicate is something that 'determines a thing', or 'is added to' or 'enlarges' our concept of the subject. The purpose of a real predicate is to provide some extra – and useful – information about the car and is, therefore, a real predicate. You could say 'the car is flimflar' in which 'flimflar' is a logical predicate, but not real predicate because it tells you absolutely nothing about the car itself (though it may reveal something about the state of mind of the utterer of the sentence!).

Following Kant's criticism, the philosophy professor **Norman Malcolm** (1911-) takes up Anselm's assumption that existence is greater (i.e. more perfect) than non-existence. Malcolm argued that it makes sense to say that his house would be a better house if it had insulation, but it makes no sense to say it would be a better house if it existed.

At first, Kant and Malcolm do appear to have a strong argument, in cases where it is already pre-supposed that something exists. For example, describing my car to you will tell you much about my car ('dirty, old, rusting, noisy'), but to then add 'it exists' seems a nonsensical remark. Why would I be describing my car to you if it didn't exist, and how does such a remark help any one else understand what my car is like? But can 'existence' sometimes be a real predicate in the sense it could tell us something that would change our idea of it? If I was to describe Superman to you and then add, 'and he exists', then surely I would be providing you with information that increases your understanding of Superman?

However, Kant would argue that this does not make the *idea* of Superman any 'greater' by saying he exists, because he is *still* an idea. The problem here is essentially a linguistic one. For example, if I were to say 'my car' and then go on to attach a series of predicates to 'my car' you would be under the assumption that 'my car' does exist. If, however, I were then to say to you that my car does *not* exist it would certainly tell you something new because I had said 'my car' not 'my idea of a car'. The same can be said about the word 'Superman' because you understand the word to refer to a fictional character. Again, if I were to say that Superman does exists then this would indeed tell you something new because it goes against your understanding of the term 'Superman'. What is at fault here is that there is a different understanding between two people of a definition of a word. You must remember that Anselm was addressing an audience who conceived of God as an existing being. However, the atheist conceives of God differently; as a fictional character.

4. THE MODAL ONTOLOGICAL ARGUMENT

You may recall that the modal cosmological argument rests upon the *contingency* of the universe: that its non-existence is a logical possibility and, therefore, there must be a non-contingent (*necessary*) cause. Such references to contingency, necessity and possibility are what are meant by 'modal'. There is also a **modal ontological argument**, which has been popularised by such contemporary philosophers as Alvin Plantinga who reformulates the argument using the concept of **possible worlds.** This idiom certainly has its critics, but it may be seen, at the very least, as a useful thought experiment that highlights the logical complexities of the ontological argument.

To demonstrate how this argument works it is best to begin by considering the **actual world** first before then going on to possible worlds. The actual world is, of course, *this world*: the one that you and I are actually living in at this moment. The feature of this world is that it is chock-full of contingent beings and events. For example, dinosaurs died out about 65 million years ago; in 48 BCE Julius Caesar became sole ruler of Rome; America declared its independence in 1776, the first aeroplane lifted into the air in 1903; Hitler was appointed Chancellor in 1933; in 1969 human beings landed on the moon for the first time. These are all events that occurred in this world. There are other facts about the world: it has one moon, it is the third planet from the Sun, and so on. Because these are all contingent, they could have been very different: this world could have had three moons, or America could still be a British colony, or Hitler might have pursued a successful career as an artist, or the dinosaurs could still be ruling the earth! All these different possibilities describe *possible worlds*. Some of these possible worlds may be only slightly different from this one, whereas others might be radically different.

Now, although all these possible worlds are full of contingent things, they also possess – like this world – necessary things. Remember, necessary truths include such things as mathematics and logic. For example, in any possible world I cannot be tall *and* short at the same time, nor can I square a circle, or make two plus two equal five. Such necessary truths, because they are necessary, must apply to *all possible worlds*. You can't have two plus two equals four on one possible world, and not on another because then it would be contingent. In fact we can use the example of mathematical truths to make an analogy with God, and it goes like this:

1. If mathematical numbers exist in this world, then they must exist necessarily.
2. Mathematical numbers do exist in the actual world.
3. Therefore, they must exist in all possible worlds.

The main point of the above is that it only requires mathematical numbers to exist in any one world (as it happens, this one) for them to logically exist in all worlds. In fact, it is not possible for them to exist on only one world. By analogy, if you argue that *if* God exists in this world, then He must exist necessarily (i.e. in all possible worlds). This in itself is nothing controversial, because it rests on the *'if'* premise and so far there is no reason to believe that God *does* exist in this world.

However, it may certainly be *possible* for God to exist because it is not a logical contradiction for this to be the case (unlike me being tall and short at the same time). In other words:

1. It is not a logical contradiction for God to exist on any possible world.
2. If God exists on any possible world, then he must exist necessarily.
3. Therefore, God must exist on all possible worlds, including the actual world.

Since God cannot be merely contingent, then the possibility of his existence on any possible world must mean that, like mathematical numbers, He exists on all worlds. Of course, the argument still rests on the definition of God as a necessary being, and that God's existence is analytic.

However, there is an atheist retort that follows the same logical structure:

1. It is not a logical contradiction for God to not exist on any possible world.
2. If God does not exist on any possible world, then He does not exist necessarily.
3. Therefore, God does not exist on any possible worlds, including the actual world.

God's non-existence as also not self-contradictory. As it is quite possible that God could not exist on some possible worlds, then it must therefore follow that He is not a necessary being at all. If it is argued that God is either necessary or impossible, then it could be that God's existence is impossible.

5. UNDERSTANDING GOD

Does the ontological argument help us to *understand* God? Norman Malcolm points out that an atheist might well accept the logic of Anselm, but that in itself would not lead to a conversion. It would not, as a result, cause the atheist to develop a living faith and to partake in the activities and doctrines of that faith. As a logical argument it may have value, but unless the individual is inclined to take part in religious life it will not have sufficient impact. Of course, Anselm was not trying to convert; only to shine a torch on those who "seek to understand what he believes..." Belief, and the religious form of life that goes with it, has to be there already. It is for this reason that Aquinas was not keen on the ontological argument, as he was concerned with showing that it was possible to attach attributes to God, whereas Anselm's proof offers little more than a declaration of God's existence.

Defining God as 'that than which nothing greater can be conceived' fits within the classical definition of God and is understandable to Jews, Christians and Muslims. Professor J.N. Findlay states that this religious attitude finds it, "anomalous to worship anything limited in any thinkable manner."

In other words, God is unperceivable so it is arrogant, not to say foolhardy, to even attempt to define God in any way. In fact, even to attribute 'existence' to God makes no sense, for we cannot possibly hope to understand what is meant by 'God's existence'.

It could well be argued that perfection does not require existence in the 'real world' because reality, at least as we understand it, is limited in its potential. This is one reason why Kant was so against all proofs for the existence of God. Kant believed in 'two worlds': the world that we – as limited human beings – can perceive, and the world *as it really is* but which is beyond our comprehension. It is rather like saying that human beings have 'human spectacles' that show the world from our point of view, but that is not to say that we are perceiving the world as it actually is. In this respect, to say that perfection implies existence brings into question what we mean by 'existence'. Is existence what we perceive, or is it beyond our conception? If the latter, then what possible value is there in saying that 'God exists'?

Although considered quite complicated, the ontological argument is, in fact, very appealing once it is clearly understood. Some two hundred years after the *Proslogion*, Aquinas declared the argument to be invalid and, in the nineteenth century, the German philosopher Schopenhauer famously referred to the ontological argument as a "charming joke". However, it has caused a number of important philosophers – such as Hume, Descartes, Kant and Leibniz – to enter the debate and continues to attract the attention of contemporary philosophers and theologians.

Many now consider that Anselm's first argument has been damned by the rigorous attack by, most notably, Immanuel Kant. Today, the second argument has greater appeal for many although, at its very best, it still tells us little about what we mean by God other than the 'greatest conceivable and necessary being'. This, in itself, provides little motivation to worship God or to partake in religious life. Anselm, it must be remembered, was writing at a time when everyone belonged to a faith community that each could recognise; there was not much in the way of a plurality of viewpoints at that time. Therefore, Anselm did not feel required to examine the attributes of God beyond accepted classical definitions.

Further reading

Davies, Brian, *An Introduction to the Philosophy of Religion*, OUP, 1993. (Chap. 4)

Davis, Stephen, *God, Reason and Theistic Proofs*, Edinburgh University Press, 1997. (Chaps. 2 & 8)

Hick, John (ed.), *The Existence of God*, Macmillan, 1964. (Has readings from Aquinas, Anselm, Descartes, Leibniz, Kant, and Malcolm).

Le Poidevin, Robin, *Arguing for Atheism*, Routledge, 1996. (Chap. 2)

Thompson, Mel, *Teach Yourself Philosophy of Religion*, Hodder & Stoughton, 1997. (Chap. 4)

Quinn, Philip L. and Charles Taliaferro, *A Companion to Philosophy of Religion*, Blackwell, 1999. (Chap. 41)

Stump, Eleanor & Michael J. Murray (eds.), *Philosophy of Religion: The Big Questions*, Blackwell, 1999. (Chaps. 8-10)

Vardy, Peter, *The Puzzle of God,* Fount, 1999. (Chap. 8)

CHAPTER FIVE: THE MORAL ARGUMENT

"We have value because we receive it from a source of value. That is what I mean, for a start, by God."

(D.I. Trethowan, *Absolute Value*)

Although, like all the other arguments, it comes in different forms, the common denominator of the moral argument is that it sets out to prove the existence of God from the evidence that morality exists in the world. There are evidential reasons, it is argued, to believe that the universe is a moral one because the vast majority of people not only experience morality, but feel obliged to follow certain moral codes that are, broadly at least, common across time and cultures.

Aquinas' Fourth Way states that "there must be something which is to all beings the cause of their being, goodness and every other perfection: and this we call God." (*Summa Theologica*)

Aquinas bases his moral principles on Plato's theory of the Forms (see Chapter One): the fact that we have the idea that things are less good, noble and so on, implies that we have an idea of how such principles can be bettered and, ultimately, we can come to an awareness of the highest good which, for Aquinas, is God.

The question arises that, if it is indeed the case that there are common moral codes that we follow, then where do these moral commands come from? There are three possible options here: first, that morality comes *directly* from God, either embedded within our conscience or through a set of universal rules that are revealed to us (divine command theory); second, that because we maintain certain moral values this should lead us *infer* that there is a God (Kant); third, that our morals do not come from God *at all*, but are a product of our situation and environment (non-religious explanations).

1. MORALITY DIRECTLY FROM GOD
1.1 Moral conscience

Cardinal Newman (1801-1890) appealed to our conscience as evidence that there is a God:

"If, as is the case, we feel responsibility, are ashamed, are frightened at transgressing the voice of conscience, this implies that there is One to whom we are responsible, before whom we are ashamed, whose claim upon us we fear.." (J.H. Newman, *A Grammar of Assent*)

Here, Cardinal Newman is echoing the views of H.P. Owen who, in *The Moral Argument for Christian Theism*, said "It is impossible to think of a command without also thinking of a commander." Moral commands do not write themselves, and so they must come from the "Supernatural or Divine". However, there are two major problems here. Firstly, it is not always the case that people do feel responsibility, or are ashamed or frightened by the 'voice of conscience' or even that they have a 'voice of conscience'. Secondly, even if we do have a moral conscience, then it is a big leap to suggest that this does not stem from the 'visible world': why could not our moral conscience originate in our environment, for example because of the way we are taught right and wrong by our parents and teachers?

1.2 Divine command theory

In Plato's work *Euthyphro*, Socrates – on his way to the courthouse to face the accusation of 'corrupting the young' – meets up with a young man by the name of Euthyphro. The youngster is about to enter court to prosecute his own father who, it turns out, tied up a peasant involved in a drunken fight. Euthyphro's father, however, forgot about the peasant and, as a result, the man died of exposure and starvation.

The son, in this case, has two options open to him: does he do as the gods would command and prosecute his own father for what appears to be an act of manslaughter, or does he 'follow his conscience' and support his own father in this? Having been educated to believe that the gods know best, Euthyphro chooses the former path. Socrates, however, believed that there is a *higher good* than the will of the gods and that, therefore, it is wrong to do as the gods command if you feel there is a higher good to be obeyed. Euthyphro is effectively arguing for a **divine command theory** of ethics; that is, morality is based upon what the gods command. However, Euthyphro seems unaware of this dilemma. The dilemma the theist is presented with is that if God is the basis for morality, then either:

(a) God wills us to do what is good because certain acts *are* good.

or:

(b) An act is good only because God wills it.

Now, if the theist opts for (a) then this means that moral values are independent of God and, therefore, even if God didn't exist there would still be objective moral values. If, alternatively, the theist opts for (b) he isn't really saying anything that has substance other than the fact that 'God wills what God wills'. For the theist to say, '*that* is a good thing to do, and *that* is a bad thing to do, because God has willed it', makes the concept of good and bad weak and arbitrary.

The dilemma is further complicated by the fact that it is not always easy to determine when God is being good, and when he is being bad. In the case of the Greek gods, Socrates could argue quite successfully that the gods could be 'all too human' when it came to providing an example. The gods were frequently contradictory in their behaviour and engaged in acts of incest, fratricide, patricide, and so on that would hardly be considered moral examples to follow by the Greeks themselves. If one were to attempt to do as the gods do then there would seem to be no limits to morality whatsoever. However, the divine command theory is an important element of Christian ethics in relation to the commands of the Christian God and, it is hoped, the example of God is a little more clear-cut than the pluralistic Greek worldview. However, anyone who knows their Bible will be only too aware that there are numerous examples of God commanding such acts as genocide. For example, God commanded Joshua to "smote all the country of the hills, and of the south, and of the vale, and of the springs, and all their kings: he left none remaining but utterly destroyed all that breathed" (Joshua 10:28 –40). Or, "Thus saith the Lord God of Israel, 'Put every man his sword by his side, and go in and out from gate to gate throughout the camp, and slay every man his brother, and every man, his companion, and every man his neighbour.'" (Exodus 32:27-29).

During the Enlightenment the divine command theory came under considerable criticism. One camp argued that, though there is an objective morality that can be perceived, God is as much subject to these morals as we are. Another camp argued that there is no objective morality at all and that moral standards are human-based. In the second case, God's will is completely irrelevant to ethical standards.

More severe criticism of the divine command theory has cen-tred around the notion that, if morality is purely a dictate of God's will, then could not God choose to reverse the current state and make presently evil actions moral? For example, God could make murder or stealing a permissible act. The response to this from such contemporary philosophers as Robert Adams (see *The Virtue of Faith and Other Essays in Philosophical Theology*, 1987), is to say that what is good corresponds with the commands of a *loving God*. However, there is still the problem of defining what is meant by 'loving'. Is it 'loving', for example, to declare war against what is perceived as an 'immoral society' or a dictator? Further, this does not resolve the question of whether or not the act is loving because God does it or whether God does it because it is loving.

The Roman Catholic response to the Euthyphro dilemma can be gleaned from the decisions made at the **Council of Trent** (1545-1563). According to the decrees of the council, when we talk of God being 'good' this is not meant in a moral sense, but only that He fulfils His nature in terms of perfection. However, the problem here is that God is still considered omnibenevolent, which is good in a moral sense; otherwise we drift towards the Aristotelian God that would not be worthy of worship.

2. KANT AND THE HIGHEST GOOD

The Danish philosopher Kierkegaard emphasised the individual and his or her relationship with God. In this case, morality is a case of obeying God's will and, for Kierkegaard, this may well conflict with what we understand by ethics. For example, in the biblical story (Genesis 22) Abraham was duty-bound to sacrifice his son Isaac because God willed him to do so, although this appears to fly against what we would normally consider 'moral'.

The question is then raised as to where our sense of morality comes from if not from God? Can we then speak of morals as being in any way objective?

Immanuel Kant has made an important contribution towards the moral argument, although it should be noted that Kant is not really presenting a moral *argument*, because he did not believe it is actually possible to prove that God exists through argument. Rather, God is a *postulate* (that is, a suggestion or, more strongly, an assumption that must be made) of pure reason. His approach goes something like this:

1. The universe is fair and human beings are free.
2. All humans desire *summum bonnum* (the Highest Good).
3. That which is desired must be achievable.
4. In this world, the vice-ridden often prosper and the virtuous are often unhappy.
5. Therefore, a postulate of life after death in which unfairness is remedied and *sunnum bonnum* achieved.

We need to examine each of these individually:

(1) Kant believed that the universe is a moral one. In other words, concepts of good and bad have actual 'weight'. To illustrate, it is often argued that the Second World War was a just war because the Allies were fighting against evil (i.e. Hitler and the Nazis). However, if there is no such thing as good or evil, then there can be no such thing as a just war; there is no moral justification for one society to interfere or make judgements over another. For Kant this is simply unacceptable; there must be a universal right and wrong. This is an extremely difficult issue that has much contemporary relevance: for example, consider the rights of other nations to pursue their own policies, even if such organisations as the United Nations consider it immoral

It is very comforting to know that the universe is ultimately a good place to live in. Stories tell us again and again that qualities such as honesty, equality, integrity, fairness, justice, respect, etc. are 'higher' than, say, greed, dominance, and violence. What is suggested here is that what we understand as 'good' is a universal law in the same way that $2 + 2 = 4$, and that these universals have their origins in the divine. Therefore, from the rational point of view, we have a duty to pursue the 'good'.

Kant also argues that the universe is free. If we feel obliged to fulfil a certain moral duty, then we must have the freedom to fulfil it. Kant does not set out to prove that we are free for, again, he argues that such a thing cannot be proven. We have to assume freedom because, otherwise, morality cannot get off the ground.

(2) The *summum bonum*, or 'highest good', is the achievement of moral perfection and happiness. Here Kant is reflecting upon our moral experience which shows that we feel under an obligation to achieve goodness; not merely an 'average' level of morality, but the highest standard possible. More than that, we also desire happiness and that virtue should be rewarded by happiness. It would not be rational to pursue virtue if it causes us to be miserable.

(3) This refers to Kant's argument that 'ought implies can'. That is, an obligation that you ought to do something implies that it is

possible for you to be able to achieve it. I would not oblige you to jump out of a ten-storey building and fly into the air unless you could do this.

(4) In this world it is not possible to achieve the *summum bonum*. Even if we are able to be perfectly moral, it is not possible to coincide this with perfect happiness.

(5) To Kant it seemed irrational that we should be obliged to aim for what is an impossible goal. Faced with such a logical contradiction, Kant is compelled to postulate immortality: if we are unable to achieve the *summum bonum* in this life, then we must be able to attain it in some future life. It is certainly not within our power to do this, therefore there must be a God.

Kant relies upon the concept of duty for its own sake, not because we are told by our peers, or for our own happiness. Duty comes before our inclinations. We might be inclined to do evil, but our knowledge of what is good requires us to do good. In other words, morality is a force that demands the Highest Good. This force is God, and it is the will of 'goodness' that pervades the universe. For Kant, it is not religion that grounds morality, but morality that grounds religion. The moral law is rooted, first and foremost, in rationality and is independent of whether or not you believe in God. Through the voice of reason, people know that they are subject to a moral law and the human agent is faced with the decision whether to obey that law or not.

Kant isn't so much *asserting* the existence of God but, using his own words, *postulating* his existence. To many, it seems difficult to be a truly good moral person if we do not believe that the world is a good place, if it is just an uncaring, indifferent universe. He considered belief in God to be a positive motivating force.

Kant argues that we have an idea of 'the best world', a vision of utopia, and, therefore, that is what we have a moral duty to aim towards. This all seems very Platonic. When we talk of morality moving from the state that it was in when we had slavery and inequality to our present position, we believe that our morality has progressed. But progressed towards *what* exactly? You cannot progress towards something when there is no 'something' to aim for. However, why would this 'aim' be God? Kant seems to say that, as humanity is not the cause of the universe and, therefore, not the cause of the goodness that pervades the universe, then there must be a virtuous 'causer'. Yet Kant rejected all other proofs for God's existence because he thought human reason is too limited in itself to provide proof for the existence of God. Remember, Kant was not trying to prove God's existence as such, rather presenting the much more subtle view that it is rational to postulate God's existence.

However, the whole 'argument' is based on many assumptions that are not demonstrable, nor does it seem necessarily rational to accept the postulate that there must be a God.

Kant is making major assumptions in supposing that the universe is fair, and that we are free. Neither are demonstrable. It may well be the case that some alien being will land on planet earth and wipe out the human race without the act even entering its moral arena. Why should we suppose that an alien would share our moral standards and respect our right to exist? Further, Kant was only too familiar with the problems of causation and freedom that led him to talk of two worlds: the **world of phenomena**, which we can perceive and inhabit, and the **world of noumena**, which is the realm of God, freedom and pure reason. We are tied to the world of phenomena, yet by exercising reason we can get closer to God and freedom. For Kant there were three kinds of life: the animal which resides in the world of instinct and causation, God who resides in pure reason and freedom, and Man who lies somewhere in-between and can choose to be like the animal or like God. The existence of the noumenal cannot be proven, and has been rejected by a number of Kant's successors such as Hegel and Nietzsche.

Further, it is not evident that all people do desire the *summum bonum*. Many seem quite satisfied with a degree of happiness and virtue. Nor is it really evident that we can achieve *summum bonum*; just because it may be logically possible, it does not follow that it is humanly achievable.

Finally, as Brian Davies points out,

> "We…might ask why the Highest Good cannot be realised by something more powerful and knowledgeable than human beings but less powerful and knowledgeable than God. Why cannot a top-ranking angel do the job?" (Brian Davies, *Introduction to the Philosophy of Religion*)

3. NON-RELIGIOUS EXPLANATIONS

The Platonic philosopher and novelist **Iris Murdoch** (1919-1999) saw ample reason to believe in the idea of the Good without committing oneself to the belief in a God. Also, many in contemporary society may well balk at the suggestion that a person cannot be both morally good and an atheist. If we are pre-

emotivism

pared to accept that there is some kind of metaphysical Idea of the Good and that, therefore, morality does have some objective basis, why should we then be obliged to base this in a God?

Our feelings of moral conscience could well be a product of our cultural evolution, a product of the brain that acts as a kind of safety mechanism that ensures the survival of a species that forms societies which leads to close contact with others. The psychoanalyst **Sigmund Freud** (1856-1939) supports the view that our feelings of Kantian duty are a product of both human nature and social conditioning. It must be remembered that despite Kant's attempt to develop a philosophy divorced from God, Kant's parents were adherents of pietism, which is a tendency of the Lutheran church. Kant's philosophy is imbued with Protestant Christianity, especially the emphasis he places on the fulfilment of duty.

Of course, it may well also be the case that there is no such thing as objective morality at all. The fact that moral conscience can differ from one individual to another suggests this. Many moral theories argue that morality is a product of **cultural and moral relativism**: each society teaches its young what is 'right' and 'wrong' which results in our feelings of guilt when we do 'wrong'.

Another account, usually referred to as **emotivism**, argues that moral properties are a reflection of our feelings of approval or revulsion. For example, the moral doctrine 'killing is wrong' is not based on any kind of objective, universal moral law, but on the common human feeling of revulsion, pity etc. that accompanies killing (killing of humans and cute looking animals at any rate). The theist may respond to this by arguing that God made us in such a way so as to be sickened by killing; it is within our nature and God is the creator of nature. However, to say that our moral psychology is a product of God seems less plausible than arguing that it is a biological product of **social evolution**: in order for societies to survive we have evolved a certain moral sense. A society would hardly last for very long if it was considered ethical and pleasing to kill each other! Although the theist may respond that God controls the mechanisms of social evolution, we seem then to be drifting away from God as having any central role in morality.

Further reading

Cole, Peter, *Philosophy of Religion,* Hodder & Stoughton, 1999. (Chap. 5)

Davies, Brian, *An Introduction to the Philosophy of Religion,* OUP, 1993. (Chap. 9)

Le Poidevin, Robin, *Arguing For Atheism,* Routledge, 1996. (Chap. 6)

Quinn, Philip L. and Charles Taliaferro, *A Companion to Philosophy of Religion,* Blackwell, 1999. (Chap. 44)

Stump, Eleanor & Michael J. Murray (eds.), *Philosophy of Religion: The Big Questions,* Blackwell, 1999. (Chaps. 45-47)

Thompson, Mel, *Teach Yourself Philosophy of Religion,* Hodder & Stoughton, 1997. (Chap. 4)

Chapter Six
THE ARGUMENT FROM RELIGIOUS EXPERIENCE

"Three years ago ... I ate seven of the so-called 'sacred mush-rooms' which had been given to me by a scientist from the University of Mexico ... I was whirled through an experience ... which was above all and without question the deepest religious experience of my life."

(Timothy Leary, *The Religious Experience: Its Production and Interpretation*)

By 'experience' we usually mean an event or occurrence that a person lives through as an observer or a participant. In this sense, we all have 'experiences', otherwise we would be saying that we do not live through events or occurrences! However, there are, of course, different types of experience. For example, you can experience 'coldness' by putting your hand into a bucket of icy water, or you can experience laughter by watching a funny movie. What typifies experience is that you are making use of your senses. This is something an empiricist (someone who relies upon observation and experience of the world in order to obtain knowledge) would recognise as providing meaningful knowledge of our world.

Another kind of experience is if, say, you are in a room of people and you sense 'friction' between two people. The latter kind of experience cannot be directly touched, smelt, seen, heard, or tasted but you can still express it to someone else in the room and they might say, "Yes, I experienced that too." The empiricist would argue that you are basing this judgement upon previous experiences of, for example, how people respond (facial expressions, body language, etc) to each other when they've had an argument. Yet how does this latter experience differ from one person saying, "I can sense God's presence" and the other saying, "Yes, I experienced that too"? Both people do seem to be sharing a common knowledge and understanding of what is being sensed. Yet an empiricist would likely as not deny that this is true knowledge. Why is 'friction', 'awkwardness', 'hostility', 'embarrassment' and any more credible and acceptable to empirical scrutiny than 'God's presence', 'God's love', or 'the holy spirit'? We need to consider in what way religious experience is distinctive from other forms of experience, and to what extent (if at all) such experiences can be related to an object outside of the person engaged in the experience.

This argument differs from those considered so far in that it relies upon **direct experience**. For example, if I were to claim that a large bear came into my kitchen and ate my porridge you would likely as not disbelieve me unless I could provide evidence. An **indirect experience** of this event might be the empty porridge bowl, bear droppings on the kitchen floor, and a large bear-shaped hole in the garden fence. However, this kind of experience – like the experience we have with the teleological and cosmological arguments – is after the fact and is always going to be more unreliable than seeing the bear yourself. To see the bear eating away at the porridge is, therefore, an example of a direct experience, and this is what is meant by religious experience.

The argument from religious experience has grown in popularity in recent years as more people appeal to their own experiences of something 'other' to strengthen their beliefs. Frequently, such experiences are not attached to traditional religious beliefs but stem from newer religious movements or to an attachment to Eastern traditions. Indeed, the more orthodox religious traditions have in the past been suspicious of claims of direct religious experience and tend to place such claims on the periphery of faith. Another reason for its appeal is its timeless element, as it is not in any way dependent upon medieval scholastic debate.

1. TYPES OF RELIGIOUS EXPERIENCE

In *The Existence of God*, Richard Swinburne categorises religious experience into five different types, two of which are within the 'public' realm, and three within the 'private'. Although dividing experiences into 'public' and 'private' is helpful in some respects, it should be borne in mind that such distinctions are not always clear cut in that we cannot always be sure that what someone is experiencing is a public event or something entirely internal.

A public religious experience could be something as simple as the blooming of a flower or the rising of the sun. Such events, though by no means uncommon, are perceived as acts of God rather than explained away by science.

Another type of public experience is one that seemingly defies the laws of nature. Biblical examples include the turning of water into wine, Jesus bringing the dead back to life, or the parting of the Red Sea that, apparently, was witnessed by over a million people and lasted several hours. Such breaches in nature are what are usually referred to as **miracles** (the next chapter will be devoted to this topic), although as we shall see such a definition has its limitations.

The first type of private religious experiences are those that are subject to description through everyday language. There are many examples of this form of experience: Moses and the burning bush, Paul on the road to Damascus, visions of the Virgin Mary, Muhammed's vision of the Angel Gabriel. These experiences in particular constitute the core of much religious belief.

A second form of private experience cannot be described in everyday language. These often come under the category of **mystical experience** (see Section 3 below).

Finally, Swinburne refers to a third kind of private religious experience which, in fact, is not a specific experience as such but more of a constant, or regular, feeling that God is simply 'there'.

When we are attempting to determine whether or not a religious experience provides sufficient proof for the existence of God, much depends upon which kind of religious experience we are talking about. For example, a public experience would be easier to verify than a private one simply because there are more people present. If thousands of people saw a flying saucer land in Central Park and TV cameras broadcasted the event to billions of others, then we would be more inclined to believe it had occurred. Of course, it is quite possible that we are all being deceived in some way, but if we are to accept experience as a basis for what we know, then we cannot easily reject the overwhelming evidence of experience. A retort here is that there are also public occurrences of religious experience. In the case of Jesus raising the dead, or the feeding of the five thousand, however, we have only the Bible to rely upon. There are no living witnesses to these events, and, alas, cameras had not yet been invented. Of course, there have been more recent incidences of a number of people claiming religious experience at once, such as visions of the Virgin Mary. However, again, the evidence is still slim: there has been nobody to video the event, and the number of witnesses – let alone reliable, objective witnesses – would not be enough to hold up the claims in court.

In what follows, we shall consider in more detail some of these different types of experience.

2. EVERYDAY LANGUAGE: PAUL'S DAMASCUS EXPERIENCE

I want to consider one particularly famous example of a religious experience: that of Paul. Paul is also known by what was his Hebrew name, Saul, and was later sainted as one of the great fathers of the Christian faith. His example is worth considering in some depth because it is representative of religious experience in many ways and could tell us much about religious experiences more generally. Below is one biblical account of the event:

> "As Saul was coming near the city of Damascus, suddenly a light from the sky flashed around him. He fell to the ground and heard a voice saying to him, "Saul, Saul! Why do you persecute me?" "Who are you, Lord?" he asked. "I am Jesus, whom you persecute," the voice said. " But get up and go into the city, where you will be told what you must do." The men who were travelling with Saul had stopped, not saying a word; they heard the voice but could not see anyone. Saul got up from the ground and opened his eyes, but could not see a thing. So they took him by the hand and led him into Damascus. For three days he was not able to see, and during that time he did not eat or drink anything.' (*The Good News Bible*, Acts 9: 3-9)

This is certainly a very powerful account, and the experience obviously had a huge psychological and physical (he was blind for three days) effect upon Paul. However, today many would doubt that Paul did actually see Jesus. If he did see something, it would be tempting to describe his experience as hallucinatory. The main question we ask ourselves today is: is this account **veridical**? That is to say, was there actually an object outside of Paul's mind (in this case, the object being Jesus) that had actual existence?

Now, consider this other account of a non-religious experience:

> Paula was coming near the bus stop, suddenly a light from the sky flashed around her. She tripped on the pavement and fell to the ground and heard a loud roaring sound. Just above the rooftops of the nearby shops, she could see a bright meteor heading towards the surface. The other people in the street were speechless as they could hear the roar but, from their angle, could not see anything. Paula got up from the ground, and could still see the remnants

of the glowing ball of light before her eyes. For three days, she had a headache and had to take aspirin.

How does Paula's non-religious experience differ from Paul's religious experience? Firstly, let's consider in what ways they are similar:

1. Both could be classed as 'public experiences' in that they are directed towards an external, public object. In the case of Paul, this is the figure of Jesus. In the case of Paula, a meteor.

2. Both are also 'public experiences' in that the events are witnessed by others on the scene. In the case of Paul's experience, the fellow travellers could hear a voice, but were unable to see Jesus. Was this because their view was obstructed in some way? Or perhaps they were too frightened to look up? In the case of Paula's experience, the others on the scene had their view obstructed by the rooftops.

3. However, both could also be classed as 'private experiences' because Paul's 'experience' of Jesus was different than that of his fellow travellers: he was the only one who actually saw Jesus and was blinded for three days. In the same way, Paula was the only one who saw the meteor and had a headache for three days.

How, then, do these two types of experiences differ? Why, if we are not believers, might we trust the latter account but not the former?

1. One consideration is that, in the Bible, there are three different accounts of Paul's experience (Acts 9, 22 and 26). It is suggested that because these accounts differ, this weakens the testimony. But if you read the three accounts they are actually quite *similar*. In fact, the accounts probably bear more similarity to each other than different newspaper accounts of Paula's experience would. Just imagine what the modern tabloid newspapers might say compared with the broadsheets. However, it should be added that when the Bible was completed, we cannot know for sure what was left out and the book as a whole does contain many contradictions that weakens its credibility as an historical account.

2. We might want to question the reliability of the *witness*. However, in both accounts, if we are dealing with individuals who are, for example, sober, educated and respected, then why trust one more than the other? Again, however, in the case of the biblical account, we cannot know the condition of the witnesses, or even if there were any actual witnesses present. Nor, for that matter, can we be sure that Paul himself had any experience, veridical or not.

3.Perhaps circumstances might lead you to question the reliability of the *experience*, if the light had been bad, for example. However, Paul says in Acts 22 and 26 that the event took place around midday. But why didn't his fellow travellers see Jesus as well? If their view was not in any way obstructed and they did look in the same direction as Paul, then why is it they only heard a voice? Couldn't it just be a prank involving someone hiding behind a rock with a megaphone and some fireworks, while Paul simply pretends to see Christ?

Point 3 might be worthy of some consideration, although it does raise the rather important question of *why* Paul would want to deceive in this manner. It is frequently an accusation directed towards religious leaders that they have ulterior motives, that they are conniving deceivers out for personal gain. David Hume wrote:

> "What greater temptation than to appear a missionary, a prophet, an ambassador from heaven…Or if…a man has made a convert of himself…who ever scruples to make use of pious frauds, in support of so holy and meritorious a cause?" (David Hume, *An Enquiry Concerning Human Understanding*)

We can all think of examples of people who have claimed the status of religious gurus but who have been shown to be charlatans and, indeed, it does demonstrate that certain people seem more prone than others to be taken in by such charismatic figures. However, does it then make sense to propose that all religious leaders are simply frauds, or that all those who follow such leaders are gullible? Not all doctors are good doctors, but that is not to say that all doctors must be bad.

We must keep coming back to the fact that Paul was the only one who saw Jesus, even though others were present. In the case of Paula's experience, there is a difference here. Even if the town were so small and Paula was the only person who saw the meteor at such close range, the empirically minded person could still build up further evidence, such as witnesses in other villages seeing a small light, a blip on the radar, or by finding the remnants of the meteor itself after it had hit the earth.

Of course, one significant difference between Paul's and Paula's experience is that only the former is *extra-ordinary*. Meteors do not fall to the earth as often as, say, a plane flies overhead, but they do so often enough. The fact that meteors hit the earth from time to time is not, generally speaking, disputed. Therefore,

Paula's experience of seeing a meteor is not 'extra-ordinary', 'fantastical' or 'unnatural'. Can the same be said of Paul's experience? Many believers would say that they have also 'seen Christ' (in visions and so on), so, from that point of view, it is not uncommon as a *private experience*, but these do not count as *public experiences*, that is, experiences that involve witnesses and other kinds of evidence. It is still this lack of concrete evidence that weakens the argument.

2.1. Swinburne's principles

Richard Swinburne would argue that, unless there are particular reasons to the contrary, we should essentially trust that what the person experienced is, in actual fact, what was experienced. In *The Existence of God* he presents two principles: The **principle of credulity** and the **principle of testimony**. Swinburne explains these two principles. In the case of the principle of testimony, Swinburne argues that we should not doubt what people report, provided there are no 'special considerations' such as being drunk or affected by drugs. According to the principle of credulity, we have good reason to suppose that what we see is actually what is there.

However these principles might be inadequate for the nontheist sceptic or, for that matter, anyone possessing sufficient philosophical rigour. Again, we may believe that Paul saw Jesus *provided* he hadn't had too much to drink, that he wasn't deliberately lying for some unknown motive, that he hadn't claimed on that same day to have been abducted by aliens and saved a maiden from a dragon's lair, etc. Is it, therefore, the case that there are no special considerations and that not only did Paul see Jesus but that others – who did not see Jesus and are not even believers – must also believe his testimony?

Perhaps if, indeed, there are no 'special considerations', we may be inclined to believe the testimony. But surely we can broaden what we mean by 'special considerations'. If we accept that Paul did, in fact, believe that he had an experience, can we then postulate non-religious explanations for that experience? Even if he believed he saw Jesus, the question needs to be raised as to whether there is an actual reference to an object outside of Paul's own mental state. For example, we must take account of physiological considerations: could Paul have had temporal lobe epilepsy, or tuberculosis? Both of these can trigger hallucinations. After all, in his letters he speaks of being weakened by a "thorn in the flesh" (2 Corinthians 4:10; 12:7 and Galatians 4: 13-14). Being blinded by a bright light and falling to the ground is one symptom of a bad fit of epilepsy and, as there would be no medical explanation for this condition, it would fit within the mind-set of the time to attribute this to the divine.

However, we must be wary. Firstly, an epileptic fit does not result in hearing voices or a radical change in one's way of life that involves dangerously travelling the world preaching and teaching. Secondly, the accusation that Paul's religious experience was a case of epilepsy is an attack on the credibility of the individual and has often been used to dismiss the beliefs of other religious traditions. For example, a few hundred years ago Christian writers said that the Muslim prophet Muhammad was a victim of epilepsy, thus denying his access to religious experience. However, this accusation could backfire and be used against Christian prophets and saints. Having said that, this, of course, would not concern the *atheist* and, from that point of view, is a fair criticism concerning the veracity of all religious experience.

Another challenge to Paul's religious experience is that the voices and conversion may have a psychological explanation. Perhaps Paul was delirious and hallucinating and the content of his hallucination vented his subconscious guilt about his persecution of Christians. Inner disturbances are sometimes projected onto the external, objective world so that a mental event is perceived as an external object. Sigmund Freud said that religious experience is the result of psychological need. For example, the realisation that comes to us all that our fathers are not perfect, but are fallible, human and finite, can result in projecting our desire for such perfection and greatness on to external objects and events.

We can look to physical and psychological explanations, but, even then, the theist could well retort that such explanations are irrelevant to the experience. So what if it is determined that the person claiming to have a religious experience was also physically or psychologically affected? Theists do not deny the claim that God mainly works through nature – which, after all, He created in the first place – and so it should not seem the least bit unusual that the experience manifests itself in some natural way.

When the late psychedelic researcher Timothy Leary spoke of magic mushrooms providing him with a profound religious experience it really wouldn't matter to him if you said that it was 'just the mushrooms having a physical and psychological effect' – it was still, for him, a *religious* experience. In the same way, the Buddhist could experience enlightenment through meditation regardless of the scientific and biological explanations for the experience. However, there is still the problem of whether these experiences are *veridical*, that is, whether they refer to an actual object.

3. BEYOND EVERYDAY LANGUAGE: MYSTICAL EXPERIENCE

In considering further its veridical nature, it may help to consider another common form of private religious experience. Although covering a wide variety of beliefs and practices, mystical experience possesses certain general characteristics. A seminal work on religious experience is by the pioneering psychologist **William James** (1842-1910), called *The Varieties of Religious Experience* (1902). In this work, James identifies a number of hallmarks of mystical experience:

1. It is **ineffable**. Essentially, the mystic is involved in the gaining of knowledge through mystical experience, but it is a form of knowledge that cannot be easily described or written down in a textbook. It is rather like trying to describe the taste of a banana to someone who has never eaten a banana. As a result, we are led to use descriptions and phrases that are inadequate, that, in the words of R.A. Gilbert, in *The Elements of Mysticism*, 'serve to illustrate the extreme difficulty of discussing non-empirical concepts solely in terms of the intellect.'

2. It is **noetic**. 'Noetic' means 'of the intellect', so the experience is not just an emotional one (although it can be very emotional); it also provides new knowledge, insight and enlightenment.

3. It is **transient**. The intensity of the mystical experience means that it cannot be maintained for a lengthy period of time. Rather it is an experience that comes and goes. However, the significance and effects of the experience last for much longer after the experience itself, perhaps for a whole lifetime.

4. It is **passive**. Although the mystic, through various practices of asceticism, may initiate the experience it is not something he or she is able to manipulate or control. Rather the experience overwhelms the recipient and he or she is, therefore, a passive receiver of a 'gift' from God.

What is important for mystical experience is that it is perceived as a form of union with the Divine. It accompanies a belief that there is another form of reality that is accessible by means of a particular form of religious practice, such as prayer, yoga or meditation. Undoubtedly, although 'mysticism' is often placed on the fringes of religious belief, it is, in many respects, at the *core* of religion. All religions speak of mystical experience. Take, for example, Muhammad's vision of Gabriel, or the Buddha's enlightenment.

One difficulty with mystical experience is that the term 'divine' is somewhat ambiguous. Although the features of the experience – feelings of union, comfort, intellectual insight etc. – may be common elements of mystical experience, the object from which it comes, whether it be described as 'God', the 'Divine', the 'Absolute' and so forth, does not point directly to God as understood in the Bible or the Qur'an, for example. If, on the other hand, the experience does relate to a more specific – i.e. less ambiguous – object, then it is open to the accusation of subjectivism. As the philosopher **Antony Flew** points out, religious experience seems "to depend on the interests, background and expectations of those who have them rather than on anything separate and autonomous."

When someone experiences a vision of, for example, the Hindu goddess Kali, it may come as no surprise that that person is usually a Hindu. Likewise, Christians have visions of Jesus or Mary. Therefore, the object to which the experience is directed assumes the identity of the religious belief and culture in which the *subject* has been brought up in. This, it might be argued, weakens the credibility of any descriptive account, hence the need for ineffability. We either have to accept that religious experience is, at best, related to some ambiguous 'other' which may have no relation to religious belief at all, or we are forced to relate the object to religious belief, which results in weakening the argument. Flew again:

> "...the expert natural historian of religious experience would be altogether astonished to hear of the vision of Bernadette occurring not to a Roman Catholic at Lourdes, but to a Hindu at Benares, or of Apollo manifest not in classical Delphi but in Kyoto under the Shoguns.' (Antony Flew, *God and Philosophy*)

However, to a large extent our environment governs all our experiences. When we see an object we relate it to what we know and understand, for it is impossible to do otherwise. For example, if someone introduced a television to a pre-industrial culture, the people of that culture would not all instantly agree that what they saw before them was, in fact, a television. Rather they would attempt to explain it in terms of what they knew: perhaps as some kind of exotic gold-fish bowl or as a not very good mirror.

In the same respect, a Hindu might describe the vision of a female figure as Kali, or a Christian as Mary. This is not to deny that there is something fundamentally *there*, only that it is perceived within the religious tradition of the observer. Although this may well result in ambiguity, it does not necessarily follow that it is right to deny the existence of 'something' that, ultimately, is beyond our comprehension.

However, although the pre-industrial culture cannot simply deny the existence of 'something' that they fail to comprehend, this is not necessarily helpful in understanding what this 'something' actually is. Such ambiguity does not contribute to greater knowledge or understanding and so, it might be argued, for the Hindu to see Kali or the Christian to see Mary does not contribute to religious knowledge, nor point to the existence of a God. At most, it can only be claimed that there may be 'something'.

4. OTHER TYPES OF RELIGIOUS EXPERIENCE

Miracles will be considered in the next chapter, as it is a major topic and raises some issues that are unique to it. However, there are a number of other types of religious experience that we need to consider.

4.1 The numinous

Swinburne's third kind of private religious experience, the feeling that God is there, that He has presence, was described by the German philosopher **Rudolf Otto** (1869-1937) in *The Idea of the Holy* (1923) as <u>numinous</u>. This is a way of describing <u>being in the presence of an awesome power</u>, yet also being separate from it. For Otto, the holy was something that was purely 'other' and non-personal. This other can be perceived through the rational, but also through the non-rational, through a sense of the holy.

The Jewish philosopher, **Martin Buber** (1878-1965) argued that the essence of religion is in dialogue with God. Man is aware of the presence of God, but in a much more personal way than Otto's sense of awe and otherness. Rather there is a *closeness*, and man is able to develop a personal relationship with God, what he called an **'I-Thou'** to distinguish it from the impersonal classification of objects which he called the **'I-It'**. For example, my relationship with my doctor is an 'I-It' relationship because I perceive her as a 'thing' that is there to cure me of a sickness. Likewise, I have an 'I-It' relationship with tables and other inanimate and animate objects. Our relationship with God, however, can become an 'I-Thou' relationship but it has to be based on trust and communication, not on proofs and logic. Likewise, I may love someone and, therefore have an 'I-Thou' relationship with that person, but I am missing the point if I set out to *prove* that I love that person.

Buber makes use of two Latin terms for faith: **fides** and **fiducia**. *Fides* is knowledge of God, rather like you have knowledge of how to drive a car or use the DVD player. *Fiducia,* however, is a confident trust in God, like you might trust a person you love. For Buber, true religious experience can only come from *fiducia*. However, the main problem with this is that Buber holds that *fides* and *fiducia* are incompatible, yet it seems feasible to both trust a person and have knowledge of the attributes of that person in the same way you can trust God yet also have knowledge that he is omnipotent.

4.2 Prayer

Religious believers not only hold that there is an invisible realm that is both real and divine, but that it is also possible to communicate and participate with this realm. This communication may be achieved through meditation, as in the case of Buddhism for example, or – in Western religions – through prayer. In terms of religious experience, the form of prayer that is significant is the **contemplative** type, to distinguish it from the merely **formulaic**. In other words, when we think of prayer we need to get away from the growing-up experience you may have of being told to sit by your bedside and say your prayers, or thank God before a meal, and so on. This might be a ritualistic activity lacking in sincere contemplation upon a divine:

> "Religion is an intercourse, a conscious and voluntary relation entered into by a soul in distress with a mysterious power upon which it feels itself to depend…Prayer is religion in act…." (Auguste Sabatier, *Outlines of a Philosophy Based on Psychology and History*)

Prayer as contemplation can be divided into two types. There is, firstly, **mental prayer**. These are prayers that do not use words, but are a form of meditation and contemplation upon the nature of the divine. These kinds of prayers are more *internal* in nature in that they do not require a state of affairs to occur. There is also, secondly, **petitionary prayer**. These are prayers that specifically ask for something and are *external* in that they make requests for acts to occur, for example for the cure of an illness.

The problem with petitionary prayer, however, is how making a request to the divine can actually cause the divine to act. People who do petition in this way may point to requesting for something to be done – for example to get an A grade in your exams – and this actually occurring, but it is debatable as to whether this is a result of God's intervention.

St. Teresa of Avila (1515-1582) distinguished prayer into specific stages that can lead to a mystical experience:

1. The Prayer of Quiet. This form of prayer is contemplative and does not interfere with other mental or physical functions. At first, this state may only last for a few seconds, but – in time – the state can last for many hours whilst the person continues to engage in everyday tasks.

2. The Prayer of Union. This is a more emotional and intense stage than the 'Quiet' stage. The subject, though still able to perform other physical and mental tasks, is no longer distracted by irrelevant thoughts or mental images.

3. The Prayer of Ecstasy and Spiritual Marriage. In this stage the subject no longer has control over their mental or physical state. This level is characterised by such activities as erratic dancing and **'speaking in tongues'**. The subject in this state can experience visions and revelations and the feeling of being in 'complete wedded bliss' with God.

The Prayer of Ecstasy is far removed from the thanking of God for the meal at the dinner table. Many new religious movements, described as **charismatic** churches involve forms of corporate prayer in which large groups pray aloud as the church leader uses 'healing hands' to cure illnesses. For example, worshippers experiencing the so-called **Toronto Blessing** claim to speak in unknown tongues, sometimes barking like dogs or roaring like lions. They also claim miraculous cures.

4.3 Conversion

St. Paul's encounter with a vision of Christ is one famous example of a conversion experience. Religious conversion involves at the very least a re-adjustment in one's attitude to religious belief or, at the more extreme level, a complete change from one religious belief to another or from no religious belief to belief.

In the case of St. Paul, his conversion was both sudden and dramatic, but there is a much more common form of conversion. For example, the Russian novelist **Leo Tolstoy** (1828-1910), in *A Confession* (1879) tells of his gradual conversion to Christianity. He talks of many years of depression and the temptation to commit suicide. This depression deepened until he discovered that "To know God and to live are one and the same thing. God is life." This led to a relief from depression: "as soon as I recognised that there is a force with power over me I immediately felt the possibility of life." Although at one level there is an immediate feeling of relief and happiness, this was only after many years of depression and searching for meaning.

Conversion in the broadest, including the non-religious, sense happens to all of us. We all go through periods of transformation; when certain aims and purposes were not previously a priority enter into our sphere of importance. For example, many younger people are extremely ambitious about their careers but they may undergo a transformation if they have children – their priorities change. This 'conversion' need not be religious and, in fact, William James has maintained that there are people who can never experience a religious conversion. There are a number of reasons for this: they may be extremely cynical or pessimistic about the world, for instance. Those who have a background in religion but later rejected it are often more prone to 'conversion' later in life when other aspects of life cease to be the priority and they look for meaning. As Tolstoy said himself, "Well fine, so you will be more famous than Gogol, Pushkin, Shakespeare, Moliere, more famous than all the writers in the world, and so what?" (*A Confession*)

There comes a point in life when fame and fortune loses its meaning and you look for other experiences to give life value. It is perhaps not so surprising that so many pop stars and film idols turn to religion.

Gradual conversions tend to be more permanent than sudden conversions. This is largely because a sudden conversion involves the subject knowing little or nothing about the belief they have converted to. As they gain greater knowledge of this belief they may question its tenets. This raises the question as to whether religious conversion is a purely pragmatic and psychological response to the situation one finds oneself in. Religious conversion, it might be argued, is not a result of usefulness, but has value in itself. But is this really the case? Whereas some might experience a religious conversion others will not but their non-religious 'conversion' could be equally significant to them. J.S. Mill, for example, suffered from depression for six months before making the following realisation:

"Ask yourself whether you are happy, and you cease to be so. The only chance is to treat, not happiness, but some end external to it, as the process of life…and if otherwise fortunately circumstanced, you will inhale happiness with the air you breathe." (J.S. Mill, *Autobiography*)

Mill's experience corresponds with Tolstoy's, but his transformation was not a religious one. Is this less significant? It certainly seems relevant that Mill was not brought up in a religious framework, whereas Tolstoy was brought up within Orthodox Christianity, which he rejected as a youth. In this example, it seems that religious conversion is not purely from 'outside'; an external force of God that bears no relation to one's cultural environment.

4.4 Revelation

Revelation is when the divine reveals truths. These truths cannot be known by reason alone, and are known only because the divine has chosen to reveal them. As an example, the doctrine of the Trinity in Christianity is a revealed truth.

There are two views of revelation:

The propositional view

The Roman Catholic Church, certain conservative Protestant groups, and traditional Judaism and Islam hold this view. God has revealed certain truths, or 'propositions' to humanity through intermediaries: in the case of Christianity this would include Jesus and his disciples; in Judaism Moses on Mount Sinai; in Islam Muhammad during the Night of Power. The importance of faith is stressed here and thus an acceptance of these revealed propositions. However, it is also believed that the acceptance of these propositions can be supported by human reason and philosophical proofs, and so this is faith in the *'fides'* sense.

Can the human mind passively receive knowledge? When we 'learn' something we appear subject to our linguistic and cultural limitations. For example, for me to learn a new language I have to relate it to my own language and to the objects that I am familiar with if I am to have any chance of understanding it. I cannot be given a book in a foreign language and be expected to understand it. Therefore, the reception of revelation suggests that it will be conditioned by the mind of the subject who receives it. Were these revelations correctly understood?

In the history of Christian teachings, certain doctrines that were originally regarded as revealed truths have now been rejected, for example the belief that the earth is the centre of the universe. If such 'truths' are subject to change or rejection this must bring into question the credibility of other 'truths' such as the virgin birth or the resurrection.

Further, religions differ in their claims as to what is truth. Such conflicts require some propositions to be false, but which ones?

The nonpropositional view

The propositional view was largely undisputed until the sixteenth century and the arrival of Protestant reformers such as Martin Luther who adopted the nonpropositional view. Faith here is the *fiducia* version of Martin Buber; an attitude of personal trust in the Divine. There is no need for proofs of the existence of God. Further, there are no infallible 'revealed truths' as such, but 'facts of faith' that must be interpreted by the religious community in the context of contemporary life.

Although this does not suffer from the problem of claiming infallibility, the problem with such a view is that it does not allow you to verify the truth or falsity of religious propositions as it will not be subject to empirical or evidential enquiry. If revelations are merely a matter of interpretation, then how are we to choose between them?

Further reading

Davies, Brian, *An Introduction to the Philosophy of Religion*, OUP, 1993. (Chap. 7)

Davis, Stephen T., *God, Reason and Theistic Proofs*, Edinburgh University Press, 1997. (Chap. 7)

Quinn, Philip L. and Charles Taliaferro, *A Companion to Philosophy of Religion*, Blackwell, 1999. (Chap. 47)

Stump, Eleanor & Michael J. Murray (eds.), *Philosophy of Religion: The Big Questions*, Blackwell, 1999. (Chaps. 17 & 18)

Swinburne, Richard, *The Existence of God*, OUP, 1979.

Thompson, Mel, *Teach Yourself Philosophy of Religion*, Hodder & Stoughton, 1997. (Chap. 1)

Vardy, Peter, *The Puzzle of God*, Fount, 1999. (Chap. 10)

Chapter Seven
MIRACLES

"If anyone says that all miracles are impossible, and that there-fore all reports of them, even those contained in sacred scrip-ture, are to be set aside as fables or myths; or that miracles can never be known with certainty, nor can the divine origin of the Christian religion be proved from them: let him be anathema."

(Canon 4 of Vatican I's *Dogmatic Constitution on the Catholic Faith*)

The subject of miracles is frequently placed in a separate cat-egory from religious experience although much of what we have been talking about in the previous chapter might also be classed as 'miracles'. In fact, it is rather difficult to present a clear defini-tion of what is meant by 'miracle'.

St. Augustine defined a miracle as "whatever is hard or appears unusual beyond the expectation or comprehension of the ob-server." However this definition has obvious weaknesses as it rests on the expectation and comprehension of the observer and not on the event itself. For example, the cargo cults of Melanesia and New Guinea in the nineteenth and twentieth century associ-ated the arrival of European and American cargo as a miracle, resulting in the development of whole new religious movements. They did not associate the arrival of ships (and, later, planes) with Western technology, but with divine intervention. This is an example of today's science being perceived as miraculous. But if we define a miracle as something which is relative to the ob-server then we do not have an objective standard of a miracle: what is a miracle for you may be science to me and vice-versa.

1. MIRACLES AS A TRANSGRESSION OF THE LAWS OF NATURE

David Hume provides a clearer definition in Chapter Ten of *Enquiry Concerning Human Understanding.* "A miracle may be accu-rately defined as a transgression of a law of nature brought about by a particular volition of a Deity, or by the interposition of some invisible agent."

We can, I imagine, all think of such miracles from religious traditions. As we have already mentioned, the Bible is full of such occurrences. In actual fact, we don't have to go back so far in time for the claims of miracles. In the past few years, numerous reports of miraculous events have been recorded. For example, in 1995 hundreds of people besieged a Hindu temple in North London because devotees had claimed to witness marble idols drinking milk that they had offered. As the chairman of the temple said, "When we tried feeding spoonfuls of milk to the gods, the milk disappeared within seconds; and it has been happening all day." (*Daily Telegraph*, 22 September 1995). This 'miracle' then, apparently, proceeded to spread to other temples around the world. A year later, an icon of Jesus in Bethlehem's Church of the Nativity was seen winking and weeping red tears. This event occurred over a number of weeks and was officially declared a miracle by the Greek Orthodox Church. (*Daily Telegraph*, 29 November 1996). Of course, in many cases, it may not be the events themselves that are so remarkable, but the timescale in which they are achieved. For example, a man may be cured of a crippling disease, but not in a matter of seconds!

We should look at the definition of miracle given by Hume, and the problems associated with it, a little further. Firstly, you may recall that Hume attacks many of the assumptions of religious belief, based on his own empirical view of the world. That is to say, if empirical evidence is contrary to a belief, then that belief should be dismissed. He applies this principle to his definition of miracles. We need to balance the belief in miracles with evidence to the contrary to determine which is the best explanation:

> "A miracle is a violation of the laws of nature; and as a firm and unalterable experience has established these laws, the proof against a miracle, from the very nature of the fact, is as entire as any argument from experience can be possibly imagined." (David Hume, *An Enquiry Concerning Human Understanding*)

Ultimately, Hume considers that natural law can be depended upon more than its breaking. Therefore, his argument goes something like this:

1. A miracle can be defined as a transgression of the law of nature.
2. We need to use the effective tool of empirical research to determine if laws of nature can be broken.

3. Our experience is heavily tilted towards the view that natural laws are not broken: when people die they do not rise again; water cannot be turned into wine.
4. Therefore, we have no rational justification for believing in miracles.

What determines what we accept as a law of nature is experience. We know through regular observation that the sun rises every morning (even if, in Britain at least, we see it rarely) and that stones sink when thrown into water. However, if one day you threw a stone into water and it floated then it may not be the case that a miracle – a break in the laws of nature – has occurred. Rather it is our failure to understand natural law. The philosopher **John Hick** defines natural laws as "generalisations formulated retrospectively to cover whatever has, in fact, happened." The floating stone would require us to looking at the circumstances that caused it to float; perhaps the sun was particularly hot that day, or the wind particularly strong, or the water salty, or a combination of all these factors and many more. In other words, we need to re-assess our understanding of natural law, not simply declare 'it's a miracle!'

Hick has a good case here. Things that are considered impossible today may be achievable in the future. For example, we may be able to travel faster than light one day. If this were to be achievable then it would require a radical re-thinking of the laws of nature as they stand, but we would not declare that each time we travel faster than light we are performing a miracle.

David Hume presents a strong criticism of the belief in miracles, and his main points can be outlined here.

First, Hume responds to the defence that many miracles, such as the parting of the Red Sea, or the feeding of the five thousand, had plenty of witnesses to the event:

> "No testimony is sufficient to establish a miracle unless the testimony be of such a kind, that its falsehood would be more miraculous..." (David Hume, *An Enquiry Concerning Human Understanding*)

Which provides the greater evidence? That people die and remain dead, or that they come back to life? Empirically speaking, miracles are so rare and so poor in evidence that they are far outweighed by occurrences of natural law. In fact, for a natural law to be shown to be false would actually be a miracle in itself.

Second, there has never been:

"...in all history, any miracle attested by a sufficient number of men, of such unquestioned good-sense, education and learning, as to secure us against all delusion in themselves; of such undoubted integrity, as to place them beyond all suspicion of any design to deceive others..." (David Hume, *An Enquiry Concerning Human Understanding*)

As we saw in the previous chapter, Hume made the point that many who claim to have seen a miracle (such as St. Paul) may be 'pious frauds'. Most of those who claim to have seen or performed miracles are, Hume argues, not beyond 'undoubted integrity' and we should rather be suspicious of the person making the claim than to believe the claim itself.

Third, accounts of miracles have a psychological basis in those who claim to experience it:

"The passion of surprise and wonder, arising from miracles, being an agreeable emotion, gives a sensible tendency towards those events, from which it is derived...the gazing populace, receive greedily, without examination, whatever soothes superstition, and promotes wonder." (David Hume, *An Enquiry Concerning Human Understanding*)

Therefore, we desire to experience the wonder and want to believe, ignoring the facts. Not only do people make fraudulent claims to miracles, but they also have a ready and gullible audience.

Hume's fourth point is that,

"In matters of religion, whatever is different is contrary...It is impossible the religions of ancient Rome, of Turkey, of Siam, and of China should, all of them, be established on any solid foundation." (David Hume, *An Enquiry Concerning Human Understanding*)

The differing claims of the many religions result in them being mutually exclusive. Miracles are often presented as proof to the claims of religious belief, but if beliefs differ so much from one religion to another, then it only results in claims cancelling each other out.

1.1 A response to Hume's criticisms

Although Hume's criticism are certainly very strong, it is possible to identity some flaws in his arguments

1. Hume's first criticism is that miracle accounts would need to outweigh the evidence in favour of natural accounts for them to be given any credence. However, the very nature of miracles is that they are rare and remarkable events. We are not faced with the choice of either accepting established law on the one hand or accepting the miraculous on the other. Hume says that we must accept or reject occurrences based upon our past experience. However, many events that have occurred due to scientific advances would, therefore, have to be rejected as 'not occurring' based upon our past experience of them not occurring.

2. Hume's second argument that there has never been a "sufficient number" of men of integrity to support claims of miracles raises the question of what is understood to be a 'sufficient number'. Further, he does not explain what is actually at fault with those who make miracle claims. Who in this world would qualify as having "unquestioned good sense, education and learning" and "undoubted integrity"?

3. Miracles by definition provide a "passion of surprise and wonder". However, these are not always of an agreeable nature to the receiver of the miracle. For example, the phenomenon of the **stigmata**, which is the reproduction of the wounds of Christ on the cross. This can be an extremely painful and long-term experience. There have been cases reported of people losing a great deal of blood because of the spear wound in the chest.

4. Finally, Hume argues that because religious beliefs differ, then their claims to experience miracles have no solid foundation. However, this places the emphasis on the beliefs of the religion, rather than the miracles themselves which might not be self-contradictory. For example a Christian may experience a stigmata, and a Hindu may experience a vision of Kali. The fact that these two religions differ in their beliefs has no relation to these two miracle experiences which in themselves do not contradict each other.

2. MIRACLES AS WORKING WITHIN NATURE

However, Hume's definition of miracles is not necessarily the most accurate, as it defines miracles as being contrary to the laws of nature, whereas some would regard miracles as working *within* nature. Richard Swinburne provided a different definition of a miracle in *The Concept of Miracle*:

"An event of an extraordinary kind, brought about by a god, and of religious significance." (Richard Swinburne, *The Concept of a Miracle*)

This definition seems to be the most accurate in that it covers St. Augustine's definition that such occurrences are unusual, but it also emphasises the importance of religion. Hume does refer to a 'Deity', but it might also be an 'invisible being', which may or may not be religiously defined. At first, it might seem a little puzzling as to why Swinburne defines a miracle as something which must be brought about by a god and have religious significance. For, surely, if a god brings it about, then it must have religious significance. However, here Swinburne is stressing that miracles, in themselves, are only significant for those who already have faith. This is a much more modest view of miracles: not as world-shaking events that cause non-believers to convert or prove the existence of God, but as 'signs' for those who already have faith and are, therefore, inclined to 'see' such signs. In fact, Christian scriptures do not have a word for 'miracle', but use words such as 'wonder' (*teras* in Greek), 'work of power' (*dynamis* in Greek) or 'sign' (Greek *sçmeion*, in Hebrew *ôt*). Muslims, too, do not emphasise miracles so much; the Qur'an itself is a miracle that contains verses, or *ayats* (signs). The problem with such a definition, however, is that it leans towards the metaphorical: to what extent can we say that such 'signs' are real?

In fact, a theist need not believe in the literal truth of miracles to have faith, despite the prevalence of miracle accounts for certain traditions such as Christianity. The gospel stories of Christ have miracles as an integral part; raising the dead, feeding the five thousand, and, of course, the resurrection. Yet recently the Anglican bishop of Birmingham said that "miracles as they are narrated [in the Scriptures] cannot in the light of our modern knowledge of the uniformity of nature, be accepted as historical." Of course, although the bishop is here interpreting miracles as against nature, he is also bringing into question the literalism of miracle accounts. Rather, the significance of miracle accounts rest in their symbolic meaning. In this sense, the miracle has the aim to inculcate religious truths rather than give an actual record of historical events. For example, the story of Jesus making the blind see again is a metaphor for seeing the truth, rather than a literal tale of an actual healing.

The literalists, sometimes referred to as 'fundamentalists' (although that term often has negative connotations these days), would hold that miracles did literally occur as recorded in the Bible. For them, miracles are deliberate 'signs' that are suited to the historical and cultural climate of the time. For a miracle to occur in, say, Jesus' time would leave its audience in a state of greater understanding of the meaning of religion and of the majesty of God, and so on. In our modern sceptical world, however, if we saw a miracle we would either simply doubt that it had occurred, put it down to mass delusion, or attempt to find a scientific explanation for the occurrence. This has led some theists to declare that we do not experience miracles so much these days as we are undeserving of them.

2.1 Miracles as coincidence

R.F. Holland stated that "A coincidence can be taken religiously as a sign and called a miracle." Holland tells the story of a child riding in a toy car across a railway crossing. The car gets stuck in the railway lines as a fast train approaches. At that moment, the train driver collapses and releases the dead man's handle causing the train to come to a sudden halt inches away from the child. By Holland's definition this would be classed as a miracle. However, an obvious criticism here is that remarkable coincidences do indeed occur in nature, but, as Hume states, "Nothing is esteemed a miracle, if it ever happens in the common course of nature" if only because we are forgetting all the times a child strays onto the tracks and is promptly hit by a train! Coincidences *do* happen, but more often they *do not* and, in other cases, they are not evidence of a supernatural force at work.

A final objection concerning miracles concerns the seeming arbitrariness of God's actions. It touches upon the whole issue of why God sees fit to cause miracles to occur at all. Although it might well be seen as a useful method of communication – Jesus performing miracles provided additional credence to his status – it does raise the question of God's supposed characteristics of justice, compassion and impartial goodness. Healing one person who is sick seems, on the face of it, all very well for that one person but why does God then seem to ignore the millions of others who are dying? However, this may well be missing the point when seen in a more holistic sense. If God is to be understood as existing outside of time, then His actions should not be explained on an event-by-event basis, but rather within the context of maybe thousands, or millions, of years. For example, Jesus raising one person from the dead might, as an isolated incident, seem somewhat unfair on all those others who don't particularly like being dead. However, this does not take into account how important Jesus has become for millions of people and the effect that has had on their lives.

Further reading

Davies, Brian, *An Introduction to the Philosophy of Religion*, OUP, 1993. (Chap. 10)

Davis, Stephen T., *God, Reason and Theistic Proofs*, Edinburgh University Press, 1997. (Chap. 7)

Hume, David, *An Enquiry Concerning Human Understanding*, various publishers, Chapter X 'Of Miracles.'

Quinn, Philip L. and Charles Taliaferro, *A Companion to Philosophy of Religion*, Blackwell, 1999. (Chap. 46)

Swinburne, Richard, *The Concept of Miracle*, Macmillan. (1970)

Thompson, Mel, *Teach Yourself Philosophy of Religion*, Hodder & Stoughton, 1997. (Chap. 6)

Vardy, Peter, *The Puzzle of God,* Fount, 1999. (Chap. 10)

Chapter Eight
FAITH AND REASON

"I do not seek to understand that I may believe, but I believe in order to understand."

(St. Anselm, *Proslogion*)

What is faith? The word is frequently used in a secular sense, for example, to have faith in the British legal system, or faith that your football team will do well this season. To some extent, therefore, faith is regarded as lacking certainty and is distinct from what we usually refer to as knowledge. You cannot know for sure that your team will not be relegated. The term, in this respect, is synonymous with 'trust' or 'confidence' and indicates a lack of sufficient evidence, or any evidence at all, for that matter. However, to say someone has faith in God seems to be making much more of a claim to knowledge than in the secular sense.

To an extent, all the arguments put forward so far are an attempt to show that belief in the existence of God is in some way rational. However, certain philosophers, such as Søren Kierkegaard, have argued that rationality has little to do with it: what matters most of all is faith, which is, quite simply, an irrational commitment. Other philosophers, notably Immanuel Kant, have emphasised that it is through the power of reason that the existence of God can be postulated. What we will examine in this chapter is the relation between reason and faith and the role of reason in determining the existence of God.

1. THE RELATION BETWEEN FAITH AND REASON
1.1 Thomas Aquinas

Thomas Aquinas, notably in his encyclopaedic works *Summa contra Gentiles (Against the Errors of the Infidels)* and Book II of *Summa Theologica*, provides an account of the nature of faith and its relation to reason. For Aquinas, human reason can tell us certain things about God. For example, he uses his 'Five Ways' to show that God exists. However, there are also certain truths about God that are inaccessible to human reason. In other words, human reason has its limitations and is also subject to error. For Aquinas, this is where faith comes in: through the power of faith one has access to knowledge of God, regardless of one's level of intelligence. This, of course, is very reassuring for those who don't have the time or energy to be pre-occupied with rational thought and yet also wish to be close to God.

We might normally associate faith with lacking as much certainty as reason. However, Aquinas is talking about a different kind of faith in what he called "divine things" which gives us "unshakeable certitude and divine truth" (*Summa contra Gentiles*, I, 4). In the view of Aquinas, faith differs from belief, for with faith, there is no room for doubt. Faith provides 'unshakeable certitude' and seems much closer to what we would describe as knowledge. Aquinas finds justification for his faith in Church doctrine: "The books of these prophets are held in veneration among us Christians, since they give witness to our faith." An act of religious faith is willing assent to those things that have been revealed by God. It is not strictly a blind faith because the intellect is also involved. Reason and faith work together, one giving justification for the other.

Because Aquinas emphasises the importance of "the books of these prophets", he is relying upon 'textual proof' in order to give his belief context. In other words, the Christian texts – notably the Bible – provide the evidence ('give witness') to support faith. However, Aquinas' reliance on textual evidence is no guarantee that his faith is sufficiently justified. The difficulty with a text is that it is a *representational device*. That is, the text is meant to represent the real. When you read a history book you are not living that particular history, but being presented with an account of it. For example, if I were to write the statement, "the sky outside your window is blue today", you cannot prove the truth or falsehood of that statement merely by continuing to read: you have to look out of your window to be sure one way or the other. It is not enough to concentrate solely on the above statement and accept its truth. Yet Aquinas is asking us to believe what the prophets said in the Bible because it is in the Bible. A Muslim may argue that the Qur'an, in its Arabic form anyway, is 'God made word' (as Orthodox Jews may argue regarding the Torah) and is, therefore, regarded as much more than a 'representation'. However, if we are prepared to accept that religious texts are in some way distinct from other texts and contain greater 'authority' we are then presented with the problem of which texts of which religions are the correct ones.

1.2. Kierkegaard and fideism

For Aquinas, there was no incompatibility between faith and reason. Kierkegaard, however, had less time for reason, although he didn't regard it as entirely irrelevant to religious belief. In his *Concluding Scientific Postscript* he argued that reason merely serves to help us recognise the fact that a belief in God is irrational.

Kierkegaard was critical of reasoned argument because each generation has shown that much of what it reasoned to be the case has been shown to be otherwise. Therefore, reason lacks consistency.

Roughly speaking, there are some issues that reason cannot settle. Kierkegaard is criticising those who always see their generation as having finally got it right and being therefore close to settling these issues through reason. They are always wrong. Therefore, rationality has its limits. At its very best, reasoning takes its time to reach conclusive truth. For example, we can conclude that $2 + 2 = 4$, or that the Earth circles around the Sun, or that $e=mc^2$, but even some of these may one day be proved wrong. But so far as the existence of God is concerned, it has yet to be proven one way or the other. Do we, then, wait for reason to provide the answers or do we do as Kierkegaard did and make a 'leap of faith'?

For Kierkegaard what matters in religion is personal passion, not reason or knowledge. He lived in the age of philosophers such as Hegel who talked in grand abstractions such as the 'universal spirit'. Kierkegaard has often been referred to as the first **existentialist** (although the term didn't exist at that time and he would most likely have been against being part of any '-ism') in that he was concerned with the individual, regardless of the grand theories of the universe that seemed to be submerging the concept of the individual. He realised that faith was illogical, but what he was more concerned with was the *psychological*.

> "The thing is to understand myself, to see what God really wishes me to do; the thing is to find a truth which is true for me, to find the idea for which I can live and die."
> (Søren Kierkegaard, *Journals*)

Undoubtedly, there is much appeal to this romantic concept of the self-righteous individual against the power of abstract reason and what he called the 'public'. What Kierkegaard was concerned with was to provide meaning in what would otherwise be a meaningless world. Christian belief, such as the incarnation or the trinity, is undoubtedly paradoxical because, by its nature, it must be. It is a paradox to say that God is also the son of God, or that a God who is spaceless and timeless can be made flesh and exist in space and time, and so on. This is where the leap of acceptance comes in: we need to make such a leap of faith because rationality leaves certain core existential issues unsolved. So in order to solve them we must go *beyond* rationality.

It is obviously difficult to criticise such a view, because it does not lend itself to the standard rules of philosophy. At the very best, one may question the extent to which a person can embrace a paradox and be aware that it is a paradox (it is perhaps not so unusual to embrace a paradox because you are not aware that there is one). However, Kierkegaard is at least prepared to accept that his faith is a precarious one, rather than deceive himself that faith is unproblematic.

2. PRAGMATISM
2.1 Pascal's Wager

Like Kierkegaard, the French Mathematician and philosopher **Blaise Pascal** (1623-1662) also believed that faith ultimately comes from the heart, not reason. However, reason allows us to recognise the advantages of having faith. He argues that it is more rational to believe in God than not, on the premise that it is a 'safer bet'.

We need to make a distinction between two kinds of reason: **prudential reason** and **evidential reason**. Many of the arguments for the existence of God have been attempts to show that there are evidential reasons for believing in God. For example the teleological argument asks you to 'look around you' for the evidence. However, Pascal is concerned with prudential reason. For example, what if I were to say to you that if you believe that the world is made of chocolate I will give you a million pounds, whereas if you refuse to believe the world is made of chocolate then I will shoot you? You would certainly have a prudential reason for believing that the world is made of chocolate because it is in your self-interest to do so, even though it goes against all the evidence.

Pascal's Wager attempts to show that even if there is no evidence for the existence of God, there are still prudential reasons for believing in Him. Pascal was a mathematician, remember, and his wager (a 'bet' or 'gamble') is not dissimilar to modern **decision theory**; a branch of mathematics in which you decide to choose different actions based on calculating different outcomes. It makes sense to gamble if the payment is big enough and the cost is small enough. For example, I show you three cards, place them facedown and you have to choose which of the three is the ace of spades. In this case you have a one-in-three chance of being right. If I then say that the stake is only £1, but if you choose the right card you win £1,000 pounds you would agree that it is worth the gamble.

Pascal was a pragmatist. That is, he believed that one should uphold a belief because it has beneficial consequences for the believer rather than being too concerned with justifying the truth of the belief. In the case of the wager, the believer is engaged in a kind of cost-benefit analysis by which you add the pluses and minuses of faith and weigh them against the advantages and disadvantages of atheism.

The calculation is based on what are called 'actions, outcomes and utilities'. The actions are belief or non-belief in God and there are four possible outcomes depending of whether God exists or doesn't exist.

	Belief in God	**Non-Belief in God**
God does exist	1. Eternal bliss	2. Eternal suffering
God doesn't exist	3. A degree of inconvenience in this life	4. A degree of pleasure in this life

For each action, one can calculate a **'utility'**. The utility of belief, for example, is calculated by taking the value of eternal life (+ infinity) and deducting from it the inconvenience in this life (say -10). Infinity – 10 is clearly a very good utility indeed!

The utility of non-belief involves deducting eternal suffering (-infinity) from the degree of pleasure offered in this life (say + 10). -Infinity + 10 is clearly a very poor utility.

Comparing the two utilities, you can see that you have little to lose by believing in God and a considerable amount to gain.

However, religious belief is distinct from many other beliefs in that it involves a commitment and affects the way you perceive and act in the world: it requires *conviction*. Therefore, to suggest that it is a matter of simply converting, 'just in case', seems easier to say than to do. To pray, go to church, bring up your children within a religious tradition, obey the moral codes etc. is a considerable change in your way of life, and may prove to have been for nothing if there is no God. Further, it is rather simplistic to view the religious believer as someone who believes for personal gain (in this life and/or the next life), as it frequently involves self-sacrifice and hardship. Pascal knew this. He responded by saying that once you put yourself in the circumstances where you hang around religious believers it will in time become easier to start believing.

The wager does rely on certain assumptions. Pascal says that agnostics and atheists lose the reward of eternal bliss, but he does not explicitly say that they will suffer eternal damnation. Even so, some suffering or even no eternal bliss still makes the wager impressive. However, it is certainly assumed that God is going to reward believers and punish non-believers, whereas He may be quite indifferent towards believers and non-believers.

Further, as the pragmatic American psychologist and philosopher **William James** (1842-1910) noted, God might well take great pleasure in punishing those who try to deceive Him. God simply doesn't like cheats!

The fact is that if you believe in God as a redeemer then you believe in God already; you don't need a wager and it is not possible to calculate utilities when you don't know the outcome. Also, although you may have a prudential reason for believing in the existence of God, you can no more believe in God than you can genuinely believe that the world is made of chocolate. Suppose I had a lie detector and said that you could have the £1 million if you genuinely believed the world was made of chocolate? Would you then accept the bet, even though I could shoot you if I can prove that you don't really believe?

2.2 William James

James' pragmatism, unlike Pascal's, does not gamble on the truth of the claim that God exists, and thus that there is a chance of infinite happiness, but rather argues that faith in God provides immediate benefit in *this* life. In his early essay *The Will to Believe* (1897), James argues that we should believe in God if it is important to us, even if we have no evidence that God actually exists. The nineteenth century mathematician and philosopher W.K. Clifford refers to what he calls **evidentialism**: "It is wrong always, everywhere, and for anyone to believe anything upon insufficient evidence." *(Lectures and Essays,* 1901) Bertrand Russell echoed this when he said: "Give to any hypothesis that is worth your while to consider just that degree of credence which the evidence warrants." (*A History of Western Philosophy,* 1945) Russell, here, was responding to James' pragmatism, for James held that it is sometimes justifiable to accept a religious proposition, *even though* the proposition lacks evidence.

James claims that a proposition (for example, 'God exists') is deserving of our belief provided it can be shown to be a 'genuine option'. In other words, the individual must choose between two or more alternatives (e.g. to either believe that God exists or does not exist). By stating that it is a 'genuine' choice, James meant that it should not be simply cast aside (Bertrand Russell argued that if there is insufficient or ambiguous evidence then judgement should be suspended) but needs serious consideration. James outlined four criteria that a proposition needs to meet in order to be regarded as genuine. These are:

1. The option must be live.
2. The option must be momentous.
3. The option must be forced.
4. The option must not be decidable 'on intellectual grounds'.

Provided these four criteria are met, James would argue that it is rational to choose to believe. Let's look at these four criteria a little more closely:

1. *The option must be live.* If I am offered the choice of either continuing to live on planet Earth or taking up residence on Jupiter I am not, at present, being given a *live* choice: it is not possible for me to live on Jupiter. Therefore, the option needs to be a physical possibility. Of course, the options may not be quite so clear-cut as this; it may be a physical possibility, but might not be considered a possibility in the sense that I would not consider it as a viable option. In this case, it can be dependent upon the individual's preferences. For example, I might be tempted by the offer of living on a desert island (which is certainly a physical possibility), while someone else might consider it as refusing to "scintillate with any credibility at all." That is, it is not a possibility for *them*, because they are not tempted by it.

2. *The option must be momentous.* Much more so than Pascal, James recognises that to choose to believe or not has a huge impact on our lives. Both in our everyday existence in terms of ritual observances and so on, and in our general attitude towards the world we live in. It is not simply like making a choice between whether to go to Barbados or Birmingham for your holidays. Like the decision as to when an option is 'live' or 'dead', there is a certain degree of subjectivity here: what might be a momen-

tous option for one person might not be for another. For example, deciding to fly in a plane might be momentous for someone who has never flown before and is afraid of flying; but for many it is given little or no thought. What defines 'momentous' is difficult; though James – using the example of making an expedition to the North Pole – sees it as being an option that has life-changing potential and is a rare event.

3. *The option must be forced.* Here one must choose one option or the other: you can have vanilla ice cream or chocolate; you can't ignore both and go for the pistachio. In religious terms, you either believe that God exists, or you do not. As we will see later, however, you could, of course, still *suspend* judgement (decide not to decide).

4. *The option must not be decidable 'on intellectual grounds'.* The option must be one, James said, which "the intellect of the individual cannot by itself decide." That is, there is ambiguity in the evidence as to which of the two alternatives of the option is more probable. Whenever conclusive evidence is available, then it takes precedence and decides the case. As an example, if you are presented with the option of believing that Paris is either the capital of France or of Italy, then the evidence is overwhelming. On the other hand, if the evidence that is available in both options (e.g. 'God exists' or 'God does not exist') is insufficient to warrant a choice either way then we are justified in believing as our will or 'passional nature' directs.

> "Our passional nature not only lawfully may, but must, decide an option between propositions, whenever it is a genuine option that cannot by its nature be decided on intellectual grounds." (William James, *The Will to Believe*)

Although James is not specific as to what he meant by 'passional nature', it seems evident that it is what the pure intellect is not. It is dependent more upon such things as emotions, needs, tastes, etc. An important point here is that it does not matter whether your belief is 'true' or not, because the truth or falsity of the option is not conclusive anyway. Rather, so far as James is concerned, you have the "right to believe" if it makes you happier and more fulfilled.

You might disagree that it is down to one of two choices: whether to believe or not to believe. Why not opt for agnosticism? However, for James, agnosticism rests in roughly the same camp as atheism: it excludes faith and, consequently, the agnostic is unable to *be* religious any more than the atheist is. James, in his classical text *Varieties of Religious Experiences*, emphasises the value of experience for believers. It provides a spiritual, heightened state of awareness and peace. For James, faith was not simply a matter of going to church, or obeying a moral code. It is an ecstatic experience, hence his insistence that to disbelieve is to lose out on something exceptional. What James was trying to emphasise is not that we should believe, but rather that is acceptable to believe if you want to, because there is much to benefit from it; you don't have to choose to suspend judgement merely because there is a lack of evidence.

However, is it justifiable then to believe in other things that can neither be proved nor disproved? For example, may I believe that there are fairies at the bottom of my garden? It would certainly be a 'momentous' option if I were to believe it, and would alter the whole attitude I have to gardening. Further, the evidence against may not be conclusive. I might wish that they exist, but is this anything more than wishful thinking on my part? Is it better to withhold a view or to be gullible?

3. BASIC BELIEFS

The obvious problem with evidentialism (i.e. it is irrational to hold to any beliefs unless we have sufficient evidence for it) is that this would disqualify many of our well-cherished beliefs; not just religious, but political, philosophical and so on. Further, even our perceptual and memory beliefs would have to be regarded as 'irrational'. A person's belief that there is a God is as basic as perceptual and memory beliefs, such as my belief that I am writing this book right now, or my belief that I had breakfast this morning. Belief in God does not require good argument to support it, in the same way that my belief I had breakfast does not require convincing argument to support it.

Alvin Plantinga holds the view that a belief in God is **properly basic**. By this he means that it is not a non-intellectual response, or irrational belief at all, but as rational as many of our other beliefs. We have two kinds of beliefs: basic (also called 'warranted' or 'justified') and non-basic ('unwarranted' or 'unjustified'). Whereas basic beliefs are those that do not require arguments or evidence, non-basic beliefs do require evidence or argument. An example of a non-basic belief would be to hold that someone committed a crime; this would require sufficient evidence.

However, it is not altogether clear what beliefs are non-basic. Plantinga argues that it is rational to maintain a basic belief provided there are 'grounds' for it. However, these 'grounds' are not based upon evidence. In fact, it is justifiable to believe in God even if you accept that the arguments against the existence of God are stronger from an evidential point of view. For example, there may be overwhelming evidence that I am Roy Jackson. However, I may hold that my basic belief, based upon my memory, convinces me that I am Napoleon.

However, if this is the case, then what beliefs are non-basic? What stops me from believing that the earth revolves around a teapot if I recall seeing a teapot rise this morning instead of the sun? In which case, any belief can be immune to criticism.

Further reading

Adams, R.M., *The Virtue of Faith and Other Essays in Philosophical Theology*, OUP, 1987.

Davies, Brian, *An Introduction to the Philosophy of Religion*, OUP, 1993. (Chap. 9)

Davis, Stephen, *God, Reason and Theistic Proofs*, Edinburgh University Press, 1997. (Chap. 8 & 9)

James, William, Pragmatism. *A New Name for Some Old Ways of Thinking*, Longmans, 1943.

James, William, *The Will to Believe*, Bantam Doubleday, 1997.

James, William, *The Varieties of Religious Experience*, Penguin, 1983.

Kant, I., *Critique of Practical Reason*, Various editions, 1778.

Kierkegaard, S, *Concluding Unscientific Postscript*, trans. by D.F. Swenson and W. Lowrie, Princeton University Press, 1941.

Le Poidevin, Robin, *Arguing for Atheism,* Routledge, 1996. (Chap. 6)

Lewis, C.S., *Mere Christianity*, Collins, 1952.

Pascal, Blaise, *Pensées* (1670), trans. by A.J. Krailsheimer, Penguin, 1966.

Quinn, Philip L. and Charles Taliaferro (eds.), *A Companion to Philosophy of Religion*, Blackwell, 1999. (Chap. 44, 45 & 48)

Stump, Eleanor & Michael J. Murray (eds.), *Philosophy of Religion: The Big Questions*, Blackwell, 1999. (Chap. 34-36)

Thompson, Mel, *Teach Yourself Philosophy of Religion*, Hodder & Stoughton, 1997. (Chap. 9)

Chapter Nine
RELIGIOUS LANGUAGE

'What we cannot speak about we must pass over in silence.'
(Ludwig Wittgenstein, *Tractatus Logico-Philosophicus*)

In his book *My Philosophical Development*, Bertrand Russell said that he "had thought of language as transparent – that is to say, as a medium which could be employed without paying attention to it." Perhaps most of the time we operate the same way: language is simply there. However, although language has, in a way, always been important in philosophy (when Socrates was asking "What is justice? What is knowledge?" and so on, the meaning of these words was obviously important), the twentieth century has seen language in itself become a prominent feature of philosophical discourse.

Because of the prominence of language in modern philosophical debate, no book on the philosophical implications of the arguments for the existence of God would be complete without taking account of how language is used. Undoubtedly, the impact of critics of religious language has resulted in re-defining what is meant by religious belief and the use of such statements as 'God exists', and it is this debate and re-assessment that occupies much of contemporary philosophy of religion. Ultimately, the central question of this debate is what do we mean when you use such words as 'God', and it might seem somewhat surprising that many of the traditional arguments have failed to address this central question.

1. WHAT IS RELIGIOUS LANGUAGE?

Having a conversation about, say, the weather is nothing unusual. We talk about such everyday things all the time, and when we converse we generally follow certain rules of conversation. If we didn't, then we would have a lot of trouble understanding each other. When we speak in our native tongue, these rules tend to operate on an instinctive level. It is only when we learn a foreign language that we become aware of just how many rules there are to language.

We have to learn different rules for different national languages, but also within the same language there can be different rules according to who you are speaking to and the situation you are in.

For example, the expert politician uses political language, or certain cultures have 'respect language' used towards elders or those in authority. Everyday conversational language also has certain rules and boundaries. For example, if you meet a casual acquaintance in the street it would not seem unusual to talk about the weather, but it would come across as rather bizarre if you reveal all your innermost secrets. Similarly, it is one thing to comment on how cold it is today, but if someone was then to start talking about God, the language drifts from the 'everyday' to the 'mysterious' or the 'metaphysical'. At one time, it certainly would not have been uncommon to 'bring God into the conversation' because it was believed that such things as the weather were acts of God.

If someone were to claim to have seen a flying saucer, it seems fair game to determine whether or not the statement is true by appealing to the evidence: Does the person have a photograph of the spaceship? Was the witness sober at the time? Many do not ask the same questions of someone who claims to speak of God. People do it all the time, yet do we question their sanity or their judgement because they go to church, or pray, or believe in an omnipotent being? Religious language seems to have its own set of rules.

A belief in God can be very profound for the believer: it gives meaning and value to their lives. When someone says, "I believe in God" he or she is not saying the same thing as "I believe I have the flu". A genuine belief in God (rather than a mere tendency to respond positively when asked if God exists) implies a commitment, a particular attitude to life. To believe in God is to say something about the kind of person you are. If a person believes in a creator God then the person believes that humankind – and the world – was created by a greater being. If God is a moral God, then the believer, if he is to be consistent, must acquiesce to a belief in objective morality.

For a variety of reasons, people question the truth of such statements as 'God exists', 'God is eternal', 'God is love' and so on. We know such statements are made all the time, and yet we wonder what the real meaning of them is. That is, what does it mean to say 'God is eternal' and how is this different from saying 'the sky is blue' or 'there are dragons'?

2. DOES RELIGIOUS LANGUAGE HAVE ANY MEANING?
2.1 Logical positivism and the verification principle

David Hume asked how, if there are so many religious beliefs in the world, any one of them can claim to be true. Hume, you will recall, was an **empiricist**, as well as a confirmed atheist. He believed that all our knowledge is based on experiences. For example, I have an idea of a 'house' because I have experienced many houses. The 'house' in this sense is a 'matter of fact' because I have come to know it by experiencing it. Hume accepted that such knowledge as mathematics, logic and so on do not seem to be based on experience, but this type of knowledge tells us nothing about the world itself unless we can relate it to our experiences of the world: knowing the number '2' only has relevance when we relate it to, say, two houses.

A group known as the Vienna Circle adopted such an empirical approach in relation to language. The Circle was founded by the philosopher **Moritz Schlick** (1892-1936) who lectured at the University of Vienna. The Circle consisted of a group of philosophers, economists, social scientists, mathematicians and scientists who met regularly on Thursday evenings for discussions in Vienna during the 1920s and 30s. The group included the logician Rudolf Carnap and the economist and sociologist Otto Neurath. Consisting of around twenty members, they would meet in a dingy reading-room of the university, and would sit in a semi-circle (although 'Vienna Semi-Circle' doesn't have quite the same ring to it). There would also be occasional outside speakers.

This group were bound together in their belief that philosophy must be based on scientific method. They were against metaphysics because it gave philosophy a bad reputation for being too open-ended. One visiting speaker to the circle, the British philosopher **A.J. Ayer** (1910-1989), argued that such transcendental speculation caused philosophy to be engaged in "the over-indulgent licensing of gibberish". They developed a theory that became known as **logical positivism**, also lesser known as logical empiricism.

By 'getting rid' of speculation about that which has seemingly no ultimate answer, the logical positivists were attempting to bring philosophy within the realm of a science, because science, by its use of experiments and observation, had shown itself to be successful in the acquisition of agreed knowledge. This was an extremely bold task to undertake, and, as such, it was an important phase in the history of philosophy. Inevitably, perhaps, such an ambitious project was bound to encounter gaps in its theory.

For the logical positivists, the only *meaningful* statements are either **synthetic** or **analytic** (see Chapter Four). A statement such as 'John has brown hair' can be proved true or false and tells us something about the subject. The statement 'God exists and He is good', however, tells us nothing about the subject that can be verified one way or the other, and nor – according to logical positivists – is it analytic. (Some would argue that a statement such as 'God exists' *is* analytic, as we saw in Chapter Four on the ontological argument). It is not open to the criterion of verifiability and, therefore, is neither true not false, but *meaningless*.

Of course, there are different *degrees* of verification. For example, you might argue that the statement 'Julius Caesar led an expedition to Britain in 55 BC' is somewhat difficult to verify in the sense that there are no living witnesses to the event and, also, that documents relating to the event are rather scanty. Nonetheless, pick up just about any encyclopaedia and it would make the same statement. Therefore, the evidence – such as it is – is weighed in favour of the historical statement being true, at least until evidence to the contrary is revealed. This, in the words of A.J. Ayer, is a form of **weak verification**: there is much evidence, but not *conclusive* evidence.

It was Ayer who introduced logical positivism to England with his ground-breaking and popular work *Language, Truth and Logic* (1936). However, Ayer – who was only twenty four when he wrote his work – was later to state that his earlier work was "mostly false", and we can see why he came to that conclusion:

Firstly, by weakening verification you are opening the back door to religious language again. Ayer admitted that there are many statements that we accept as factual that, according to the criterion of verifiability, would be classed as meaningless. In fact, if nothing else, the existence of God could be verified when you die (what John Hick called **eschatological verification**).

Secondly, it has been argued that the verification theory is self-refuting. The ancient Greek philosopher Democritus (c.460-c.370 BCE) referred to a principle known as ***peritrope*** (reversal) by which philosophers take a principle and reverse it on to the person proclaiming it. The verification principle is typical of this: 'A statement is meaningless unless it is subject to the criterion of verifiability'. However, the *principle itself*, as it is not subject to the criterion of verifiability (for the statement is neither analytic nor subject to empirical proof), is therefore meaningless.

Without getting bogged down in the issues here, it is worth briefly mentioning a third consideration. The analytic-synthetic distinction is not so clear-cut in practice. Kant, for example, argued that we could have *synthetic a priori* statements. For example, mathematical statements such as 'two plus two equals four' are usually considered *a priori* (we know the equation is true through exercising our reason and, therefore, it is unnecessary to consider any other evidence to show that the statement is true) and analytic (you know that the predicate is included in the subject). Now, it is not disputed that *all* analytic beliefs are *a priori*. However, it is debatable as to whether all synthetic beliefs are *a posteriori*. For example, what of the statement '13 x 13 = 169'? It is still *a priori* because we can exercise our reason to determine it's truth, but – without the aid of a calculator – can we be *sure* that the predicate is included in the subject? In other words, we could be *mistaken*. In this sense, it could be argued that the equation is providing us with information that we were not aware of before.

Such difficulties have led some philosophers, such as the American **W.V.O. Quine** (1908-2000), to claim that there is no fundamental difference between synthetic or analytic beliefs. Verifiability is not so popular with modern-day philosophers. It may be somewhat premature, however, to reject the theory entirely just yet. **Kai Nielsen**, for example, supports verifiability as a good tool for philosophical criticism and a useful criterion for determining true and false statements. Nielsen would not say that all religious statements are meaningless, only that they are *false*. For example, the statement, 'God is everywhere' can result in meaningful, enlightening discourse, and, as such, it serves a useful function. But this is different from saying that the statement is factually true.

2.2 Falsification

In the 1950s a debate – led by Anthony Flew – on **falsification** ensued. It is one thing to say that a religious statement cannot be meaningful because it cannot be verified, but what if we say that a statement is meaningful because it can be falsified? This way, science accepts that statements can be proven to be false (i.e. the sun – in given circumstance – may not rise tomorrow) but the statement is still meaningful because it admits it. In other words, scientific statements make an assertion about the world and then challenges us to prove it to be untrue. An example of this can be found in mathematics and is known as **Goldbach's Conjecture**. This states that any even number above 2 is the sum of two prime numbers. A prime number is any whole number (an integer) greater than 1 that cannot be a product of smaller positive integers. For example, 2, 3, 5, and 7 are prime, whereas 4 (= 2 × 2), 6 (= 2 × 3), 8 (= 2 × 4), and 9 (= 3 × 3) are not. Goldbach's Conjecture states that any even integer (greater than 2) is the sum of two prime numbers. Do this with any even number and you'll find this to be the case. Now, the reason this is a *conjecture* and not a theory is because it has yet to be proven to be true. At this moment, mathematicians are using astronomically high even numbers to find out if there is a number that does not contain the sum of two prime numbers. So far, they have yet to discover such a number. And so, we *believe* this conjecture to be true, but it may be mistaken.

In this sense we can at least say that scientific statements are saying something positive and, therefore, meaningful, whereas – the theory goes – religious statements assert nothing. For example, if I were to say that 'God watches over me' then I am making an assertion that cannot be falsified; especially if I also state that God is invisible. Of course, if I then get run over by a bus that might suggest that God was distracted momentarily, but equally I could retort that it was part of God's plan. The point is that I will not allow for anything to count against my belief that He is watching over me. Quite simply, the statement I am making is 'unscientific' because I am not allowing for the possibility of falsification. The statement, therefore, is really not asserting anything at all and must be meaningless.

Flew used John Wisdom's **parable of the secret gardener.** Two explorers come across a clearing in the jungle. One explorer believes that there must be a gardener that looks after this plot of land and so they camp out to find out who this gardener is. However, no gardener is seen. Nonetheless, the explorer perseveres, arguing that the gardener is invisible, so they construct electric fencing. Again, nothing happens, yet the explorer persists that the gardener can go through fencing undetected. Despite constant attempts to disprove the existence of the gardener, the explorer will always qualify his initial claim. This is what Flew meant when he said that religious claims suffer from "death by a thousand qualifications".

A riposte to this provided by some theists is that, on the contrary, they *do* subject their claims to attempts at falsification. For example, the problem of evil (see Chapter Ten) is accepted by theologians as a genuine attempt to disprove the existence of God. However this does not prevent the religious believer from responding by way of the free will defence. The point here, according to the theist, is that there has been no successful attempt made at falsification. If it were possible to successfully falsify a statement such as 'God exists' then the *rational* religious believer would accept it. This, of course, does not take account of the *irrational* religious believer who would refuse to believe any evidence, however concrete. Equally, science does not take account of the 'irrational scientist' who might uphold that the earth is flat, or the 'irrational historian' who argues that the holocaust never happened.

Basil Mitchell supports the view that believers are aware of the philosophical problems created by the falsification principle, but that this is not sufficient reason to discard belief: to do so would be tantamount to considering one's beliefs as insignificant. Mitchell retorts with his own **parable of the partisan and the stranger**. In a time of war, a partisan meets a complete stranger who claims to be on the partisan's side and that he must have faith in him even if he acts in a manner that suggests he is with the enemy. The partisan continues to have faith in the stranger even when the stranger withholds help.

Here the partisan is aware that the behaviour of the stranger is ambiguous, and one senses that the partisan is having to wrestle with his own doubts. However, his belief in the integrity of the stranger is so strong he will not allow these pressures to persuade him otherwise.

The British philosopher **R.M. Hare** (1919 -) responded to Flew by suggesting that religious beliefs are essentially unfalsifiable but that does not entail that they are therefore meaningless. Here, it depends on what is meant by 'meaning'. Does a statement that affects a person's life have meaning or not? For the person affected it certainly does. Hare calls religious beliefs that have meaning **'bliks'**: A blik is:

> "A way of regarding the world which is in principle neither verifiable nor falsifiable – but a mode of cognition to which the terms 'veridical' or 'illusory' properly apply."
> (John Hick, *Faith and Knowledge*)

For the religious believer the existence of God cannot be simply a meaningless belief because it can give value and purpose to that person's life.

Hare gives the example of a lunatic who is convinced that the professors at his university are trying to murder him. Despite his friends' attempts to persuade him that this is not the case by showing him evidence of mild-mannered dons, the lunatic remains convinced.

It is perhaps unfortunate that Hare chooses the example of a 'lunatic' to make his point. Nonetheless we can take the point that our beliefs, our world-view, undoubtedly affects our decision-making and actions. It does not matter whether others share your 'blik' or even if it is true or false. For example, many refuse to fly because of their belief in the likelihood it will crash, despite being presented with evidence of how safe planes are compared to most other forms of transport. This belief may be 'irrational', but meaningful nonetheless. Whereas Mitchell argues that the believer does recognise that his belief is in conflict with the evidence (as in the example of the partisan), Hare argues that the person who has a blik does not allow anything to count against his or her belief.

3. HOW CAN WE TALK ABOUT GOD?

So far, we have considered the criticisms levelled against the theists that statements such as 'God exists' are meaningless because they either cannot be verified or are not subject to falsification. We have shown that there are weaknesses to such criticisms. However, if we are to argue that statements such as 'God exists' or 'God is good' are not, after all, entirely meaningless, we still need to address the issue of what such statements actually do *mean*. If it is considered that neither falsification nor verification provides an adequate criterion for establishing meaning, other ways of talking about God need to be considered.

3.1 Analogy

The issue of establishing what is meant when we use religious language has a long history. The renowned Jewish philosopher **Maimonides** (1135-1204) argued that God is unknowable and that the only way one can talk about God is by saying what He is not (this approach is what is known as **apophatic theology**). However, does saying He is *not* physical, not finite, not knowable and so on, tell us any more about what He *is*? Why not simply say that He *is* infinite, spiritual and unknowable? Sometimes it seems more comprehensible to say 'God *is* good' or 'God *is* the creator'.

St. Thomas Aquinas thought that it is indeed possible to talk about God in a meaningful way, through the use of **analogy**.

Consider the following two statements:

Polly is a parrot
Roger is a parrot.

In both statements, in this case, the word 'parrot' refers to the same thing: a tropical bird. (You can, of course, be referring to Polly the woman next door, in which case you are using a figure of speech, or a metaphor: more on that later in the chapter). In other words, the word is being used **univocally** (meaning the same thing).

Consider these two statements:

I fancy a game of cricket
In this matchbox I've got a cricket.

Now, we know you can't get a game of cricket in a matchbox, so the word 'cricket' – though written the same – means something different here. The former is referring to a game people play (and a game England frequently lose); the latter to a chirping insect. In other words, these words are used **equivocally** (the same word used in a different way).

However, Aquinas said there is a *third* way of using words; we can use analogy.

For example, when the believer says 'God is good' he or she doesn't mean it in the univocal sense (not good in the sense little Johnny is good because he ate all his greens), nor in the equivocal sense (having a completely different meaning and, therefore, still not telling us anything about God). Rather, by analogy, we can say there is some basis of comparison, because we have an idea of what good is and our ideas derive ultimately from God in the first place. It is worth bearing in mind that, for Aquinas, causes and their effects are intimately connected. God's world is a reflection of what God is; it contains his 'signature'. So, when we use words like 'good', 'wise' and 'all-knowing', we already have a reference point: our language ultimately stems from an attempt to interpret the world and the world, in turn, reflects God's nature. Language both frees us and restricts us: it is all we have. Yet it takes us some of the way in understanding, in the same way as using the analogy of the human heart as a mechanical pump does: it obviously *isn't* a mechanical pump, but it helps us to understand its operation.

So, at least we have *some* idea as to what is meant when the believer says 'God is good'. In the world, we see good acts all the time. Although we cannot say God's goodness is the same, it is much 'greater' and very 'different'. However, we also understand the words 'greater' and 'different' because we see those in the world as well.

The problem of using analogy, however, is whether such statements as 'God is good' or 'God is wise' really tell you anything about what God is like. That is, do they have anything *significant* to say? For example, to say that the attributes of Polly are that she has a pair of wings, a beak, a red tail and likes to say "Polly wants a cracker" tells us quite a lot about Polly. That is, we are presented with a series of **predicates** (wings, beak, red tail) that tell us more about the **subject** (Polly). The question you have to ask yourself is: does saying that God is 'wise by analogy' tell us anything about God?

3.2 Symbolic language

Another option is the use of **simile**, such as 'God is like a watchmaker'. One can picture a watchmaker, making his device and getting it to tick away nicely and extract from that an image of God creating the world and getting it rolling. An extension of this is the use of **metaphor**. A metaphor is frequently used in literature as it is regarded as an imaginative way of trying to express something (for example, 'his poetry is a metaphor for spiritual hunger.'). Metaphor is frequently used in religious language, such as 'heaven is a land of milk and honey'. Note here that, unlike a simile, we are not saying that heaven is *like* milk and honey. Rather, the image conjured up is an association of sweetness, warmth, security, plenty, and so on.

There is a danger, however, about saying that all talk of God is metaphorical. We know the remark 'I only meant that metaphorically'. In other words, it has an element of 'untruth' about it. It may be very poetic, but it's not really true.

Symbolic language is basic to the study of religion. Signs – or representational symbols – do not necessarily have any obvious relationship to what they represent. Consider, for example, early Christian acrostic (an acrostic is a series of lines in which the first, middle or last letters of each line make up a word or a sentence) or 'secret signs' such as the fish (ICHTHUS). More common are presentational symbols, which make a claim to represent something, especially a material thing – such as water – to represent a non-material thing – such as purity. Presentational symbols have qualities that are analogous: thus water is, in reality, a cleanser and so shares something with the notion of 'spiritual cleansing'.

The contemporary French philosopher Paul Ricoeur has pointed out that symbols are **multivalent**: that is, they carry multiple meanings that are revealed according to the way we approach them and our own life experience. We both interpret symbols, and symbols help us to interpret ourselves. To the non-Christian, bread and wine may be simply just that: one provides sustenance and the other makes you 'jolly'. To a Christian, however, they symbolise much more; they are the flesh and blood of Christ. Analogy is frequently used in an attempt to explain what actually occurs during the Eucharist, what makes the bread and wine at communion different from any other bread and wine. Again, the influence of scholastic philosophy is evident here. Aristotle made a distinction between 'substance' (the essential nature of some-thing) and 'accident' (the outward appearance of something). The theory of transubstantiation states that the 'accident' of bread and wine remain the same, whereas the 'substance' has changed to that of the body and blood of Christ.

This view was criticised by Protestant theologians. The Swiss theologian **Ulrich Zwingli** (1484-1531) used the analogy of a queen's ring. A ring, in itself – that is, without any associations – is simply that; a ring. But place the ring on the finger of a queen and its *significance* has changed, without the nature – the substance – of the ring actually changing at all. The ring now has personal associations with that of authority, power, majesty and so on. Hence the multivalent element of symbolism: for Christians, bread and wine have associations beyond their nature.

But how far can symbolism go? If we say that the Devil is not *literally* the Devil, and bread and wine are not *literally* the body and blood of Christ, then, surely, the next step down this slippery slope is to say that God is not *literally* a greater being. In fact, much modern theology is heading that way. The revisionist Stewart Sutherland speaks of Christ, not in a literal sense, but as repre-senting a *real possibility*, i.e. a life of goodness, love and unselfish-ness. To those that live within the faith communities there are archetypes to live by: Christ for Christians, Muhammad for Muslims, Moses for Jews, Siddhartha for Buddhists, Rama and Sita for Hindus. Religion consists of a series of narratives, but these are perceived by believers to be much more than stories: they are *real possibilities* and examples for people to live up to. But, for people like Sutherland, these possibilities – examples of the 'holy life' – are also the *right* life.

4. IS RELIGIOUS LANGUAGE A GAME?

Philosophers have argued that there are different ways by which language is given meaning: through the method of verification and falsification, or by determining meaning through symbol and comparison. An important contributor to our understanding of how we use language is **Ludwig Wittgenstein** (1889-1951). Wittgenstein was born in Vienna, but spent much of his life in Britain, first to study engineering at the University of Manchester, then to study philosophy at Trinity College, Cambridge. Throughout Wittgenstein's career he had a concern with the scope and limits of language.

The quote at the beginning of this chapter is the last sentence of Wittgenstein's early work '*Tractatus Logico Philosophicus*' (quite a mouthful, so usually abbreviated to the *Tractatus*). Despite his reputation for seriousness, Wittgenstein was an interesting man who led a varied life and I would recommend Ray Monk's biography of him. Also, do not be put off by the imposing title of the *Tractatus* and its curious style of short paragraphs, divisions, subdivisions and so on. It is actually considered quite literary in its way and is worth a read (it's really more of a long essay than a book). Having said that, Wittgenstein did not engage in much systematic writing, and so different philosophers have interpreted him in different ways. In actual fact, he produced two different and incompatible philosophies during his lifetime.

4.1 Picture theory

His earlier philosophy can be termed the 'picture theory of meaning'. Wittgenstein did not provide any specific examples of exactly what he meant by this. However, it can be said that he thought that a sentence is only true or false if it can be *literally* pictured and is not just a metaphor. For example, if you say "Peter walked to the post office from the station", it is possible to picture this, to even make a little model of it, where all the objects (Peter, post office, station, street, etc.) fit together logically and correctly. Sentences are often more complicated than this, of course, but they can still be broken down into simpler components that can then be actualised as models.

Where this is not the case, however, is with moral, aesthetic and religious statements. 'God is love' is not something you can construct a model of. In this case, for Wittgenstein, the statement is meaningless and should be "passed over in silence". Now, of course, you may find weaknesses in this argument, especially the idea that statements can be so readily identified as being 'pictorial' or not, and this may well be one reason why Wittgenstein later abandoned his theory and came up with another, conflicting one.

4.2 Language games

Primarily from lecture notes, we have Wittgenstein's theory of language games. By this, Wittgenstein does not mean that language is a frivolous activity. What he identified was that language operates in the same way as a game does. For example, the games of football, tennis and cricket all have different rules; nonetheless they are all defined as games. That is, they all share something in common in that they are all 'gaming activities'. In the same way, religious language is still a 'language' like other forms of language (conversational language, etc), but it nonetheless has its own rules.

The implications of this view are a form of relativism: the Football Association cannot declare that the rules of cricket are 'wrong' merely because they do not follow the same rules as football. Likewise, the atheist cannot say that the language used by the theist is 'wrong' merely because the theist does not operate under the same language rules. The best you can say is that each view is relative.

This view has implications beyond the philosophical. Wittgenstein was adopting a form of cultural relativism in which there can be no external criticism of the language. Much Eighteenth-century European thinking worked on the assumption that the so-called 'primitive' cultures that were studied were inferior and irrational compared with western civilisation. A similar approach has been adopted towards religious language: it is irrational and therefore meaningless. This is making a judgement that rationality is in some way superior and correct, whereas the language of faith has no bearing on the world. However, for Wittgenstein, languages themselves are 'forms of life' and, therefore, have meaning in themselves.

His remark, "don't ask for meaning, ask for use," suggests that the task of philosophy is not logical analysis, but the description of our various 'language games': that is, how words are used in the context of our life and culture. Religious language should not be criticised for being meaningless. In fact, it is an essential part of a community's life. Religious belief cannot be corroborated or falsified by evidence – it is immune to rational criticism. As Wittgenstein says, "Why shouldn't one form of life culminate in an utterance of the belief in a Last Judgement?"

4.3 Realism, anti-realism and reformed epistemology

Many have misgivings over seeing religious language as a 'language game', as it implies (even if it isn't meant to be the case) that it is something of a frivolous activity, that it trivialises all belief systems. Generally, believers regard religious statements as important, of having a definite value. As said at the beginning of the chapter, someone who believes in the existence of a moral God must – if they are consistent – also have moral values that not only affect his or her life, but also result in views on how *others* should lead their lives if they are to achieve salvation. For religious believers who are **realists** God is real and 'out there'. The existence of God is seen as factual and is, therefore, not subject to reinterpretation. The concern for the realist is that the more religious claims become a matter of the environment and psychology, the less significant religious assertions are seen to be.

A group of realists that can come under the general term of **reformed epistemologists** reject the traditional arguments for the existence of God because they reject the use of rational argument as providing any kind of foundation for belief. A statement such as 'God exists' is true, not because it can be 'proven' by the design argument, cosmological arguments, and so on, but because you believe it to be true. Belief – founded upon revelation, worship, prayer, morality etc – provides a clear and coherent structure for life and those who do not believe are lacking such a structure. The non-believer is a victim of pride and arrogance and of blindly depending upon human reason and ignoring God's grace. God is very 'real' and this is known through faith and revelation, rather than through the limitations of rational argument.

Anti-realists, however, believe that God is not 'real' in the sense of existing outside the religious community, but 'real' for those who believe. For instance, Muslims believe that the Qur'an is the word of God, and Christians believe that Christ is God. These are 'true' for believers, but they cannot be verified by appealing to evidence and are not, therefore, subject to proof. In fact, to talk of verification or proof is a waste of time and, in fact, does not even make sense. The prevailing climate of 'many truths or none at all' has a profound effect on religious debate. The view that religion no longer has a place in the modern 'rational world' has led many to adopt an attitude of fideism: the belief that faith does not need the support of reason to defend it. Many scientists who are religious believers find no difficulty fitting their faith within their world view, because it is not part of the 'rational debate'. Non-realists may accept the Christian story as a fiction. Writers such as Don Cupitt and D.Z. Phillips have argued that religious language is not about the 'metaphysical' at all, but is actually more directly related to our experience. Those within a faith community have their own way of using languages; their own 'religious language'. Nonetheless, embracing the fiction still gives life meaning in a universe that it would otherwise lack.

One can see how anti-realism can offer the security that realism may find difficult in today's world to defend, but it is nonetheless subject to the criticism that one truth is as good as any other. For example, the former Archbishop of York, Lord Habgood, in his book *Varieties of Unbelief*, refers to Islam's reluctance to allow internal criticism of itself and the Qur'an. Whereas he sees Islam clinging to absolutes and certainties as a weakness, many Muslims would retort that the very reason churches are emptying is because Christianity *lacks* such absolutes.

Further reading

Ayer, A.J., *Language, Truth and Logic*, Pelican, 1974.

Aquinas, *Summa Theologica*, Eyre and Spottiswoode, 1966.

Davies, Brian, *An Introduction to the Philosophy of Religion*, OUP, 1993. (Chaps. 1 & 2)

Hume, David, *Dialogues Concerning Natural Religion*, Penguin, 1990.

Magee, Bryan, *Men of Ideas: Dialogues With Fifteen Philosophers*, OUP, Oxford, 1978. (Dialogues 5 & 6)

Mitchell, Basil (ed.), *The Philosophy of Religion*, OUP, 1971 (Chaps. I, III, IV & VII)

Monk, Ray, *Ludwig Wittgenstein*, Jonathan Cape, 1990.

Morton, Adam, *A Guide Through the Theory of Knowledge* (2nd Edition), Blackwell, Oxford, 1997. (Chap. 3)

Nielsen, Kai, *An Introduction to the Philosophy of Religion*, St. Martin's Press, 1982.

Nielsen, Kai, *Contemporary Critiques of Religion*, Herder and Herder, 1971.

Quinn, Philip L. and Charles Taliaferro, *A Companion to Philosophy of Religion*, Blackwell, 1999. (Part IV)

Sutherland, Stewart, *God, Jesus and Belief*, Blackwell, 1983.

Swinburne, Richard, *The Coherence of Theism*, Clarendon Press, Oxford, 1977.

Thompson, Mel, *Teach Yourself Philosophy of Religion*, Hodder & Stoughton, 1997. (Chap. 1)

Vardy, Peter, *The Puzzle of God*, Fount, 1999. (Chaps. 4-6)

Wittgenstein, Ludwig, *Blue and Brown Books*, Blackwell, 1973.

Wittgenstein, Ludwig, *Philosophical Investigations*, Blackwell, 1988.
Wittgenstein, Ludwig, *Tractatus, Logico Philosophicus*, Routledge,
   2001.

Chapter Ten
THE PROBLEM OF EVIL AND THE FREE WILL DEFENCE

"Never shall I forget that night, the first night in camp, which has turned my life into one long night, seven times cursed and seven times sealed. ... Never shall I forget those moments which murdered my God and my soul and turned my dreams into dust."

(Elie Weisel, *The Night*)

Elie Weisel's book *The Night* is a powerful account of the Holocaust, an event that resulted in the death of five to six million Jews. The most notorious death camp was Auschwitz in Poland where around a million Jews lost their lives. As one former Polish guard at Auschwitz describes, the children were thrown straight into furnaces without first being gassed: "They threw them in alive. Their screams could be heard at the camp. We don't know whether they wanted to economise on gas, or if it was because there was not enough room in the gas chambers."

Alas, our history is full of such examples of crimes against humanity. We do not have to go back far in history for examples of some of the worst atrocities committed. The Cambodian guerrilla commander Pol Pot , as prime minister from 1975-79, caused the death of some two million through executions, starvation, overwork and disease. In 1994 there was a massacre of half a million Rwandans and a million refugees who fled the country resulting in over a thousand deaths a day through disease and reprisals. Then there was the 'ethnic cleansing' in Bosnia. The list is much, much longer. These kinds of acts which are the result of man's own actions are known as **moral evils**.

Aside from such moral evils, there are also **natural evils** in the world: the cyclone in Bangladesh in 1970 which resulted in the loss of some half a million lives; the Black Death during the Middle Ages resulting in the loss of perhaps half of the European population (in some cities, such as Florence, virtually the whole population died); the 1556 earthquake in the Chinese province of Shaanxi, resulting in the loss of 800,000 lives. Again, the list is a very long one indeed.

When we talk of evil we also mean the suffering that is the result of the evil. That is, to suffer at all is an evil. And so when we ask the question, "why is there evil in the world?" we are also asking, "why should people suffer?"

With such evil in the world, it is perhaps understandable why many religious believers have doubted their own faith in a good and caring God. Elie Weisel's declaration that, for him, God is dead was echoed by many Jews after the Holocaust. With a few exceptions, most people readily admit that there is evil in the world, and so the criticism levelled against religious believers is how the existence of such evil could possibly be consistent with the concept of an all-powerful, all-good God.

1. GOD AND INCONSISTENCIES

When we consider some of the classical theist characteristics of God (for a reminder, look back to chapter one of this book), we are confronted with a number of problems in relation to evil:

1. God is omnipotent. That is to say, God is all-powerful. But if He can do anything that He so wishes, why does He allow evil to occur? If He is unable to prevent evil from occurring, then He cannot be all-powerful.

2. God is omnibenevolent. By His nature, God is goodness; He is not an evil God. But if God is not evil, then what is the cause of all the evil in the world? How can a good God sit by and allow such evils to occur?

3. God is omniscient. God knows all there is to know. He is not ignorant of the goings-on of the world, nor, for that matter, can he be unaware of what will happen in the future, for this would put an unacceptable limitation on God. Therefore, if he knows evil is being committed, why doesn't he prevent it from happening? If He knew, for example, that Hitler would grow up to be the cause of so much suffering, why didn't He make Hitler a good man instead?

Given that evil does exist, then it must be the case that, if God exists, He can't eradicate it, and so is not omnipotent; or He doesn't want to eradicate it, and so is not omnibenevolent; or He doesn't know about it, and so is not omniscient. Whichever is true, God cannot be as he is traditionally conceived.

2. GOD IS NOT THE CAUSE OF EVIL

Very briefly, the problem of evil boils down to this inconsistency:

1. God is omnipotent
2. God is omnibenevolent

3. God is omniscient
4. God causes evil to exist

The problem centres on the accusation that propositions 1-3 above are inconsistent with proposition 4. How might the theist resolve this inconsistency?

One possible approach is to deny proposition 4, and replace it with 4a. Like so:

1. God is omnipotent
2. God is omnibenevolent
3. God is omniscient
4a. God is not the cause of evil

Provided we are prepared to accept proposition 4a as viable, then it is no longer inconsistent with propositions 1-3. However, we are then faced with the problem of how evil can exist without God being its cause.

2.1 Evil is the absence of good

The ancient Greek philosopher Aristotle stated that when confronted by two contraries, one is negative in relation to the other. For example, darkness is an absence of light; poverty is an absence of wealth; ugliness is an absence of beauty; and, of course, evil is an absence of good. Influenced by this, St. Thomas Aquinas, in *Summa Theologica*, stated that evil isn't a 'thing' at all, but is, rather, an *absence* of goodness. Evil, for Aquinas, cannot possibly be a 'thing' because all 'things' are created by God and God, being all-good, would not create evil things. It is important to point out that Aquinas does not deny the existence of evil, but that it is not the product of God. Aquinas states that there are two different kinds of 'absence of good': either the **privative sense** or the **purely negative sense**:

The 'purely negative sense' of absence of good is not, for Aquinas, an evil but rather an absence of the ultimate Good. Aquinas believed that the ultimate Good (with a capital 'G') was, of course, God and so all of God's creations are also good (for He does not create anything 'bad'), but not *perfectly Good*. For example, human beings, as part of their God-given nature, can reason, can walk, swim, talk, sing etc. However, a human being – unlike, say, a goldfish – cannot swim around a bowl all his life. A goldfish, for its part, cannot reason, walk, talk, etc. And so, we can say that mankind's inability to survive underwater indefinitely is an absence of Good. Likewise, the inability of a fish to walk is an absence of Good. It is not, however, an *evil*.

In the privative sense, evil is a privation of good (*privatio boni*). Remember that God only creates what is good. Therefore, Man's true nature is to be good. If Man does not live up to his nature then, in this sense, he is evil: *But he wasn't made 'evil'*. It also follows that if a bird has no wings then it is 'evil', or if a person is born with no arms then he or she is 'evil', but Aquinas stresses that this is not the same as being *morally evil*. We are all evil because we all fail in some way to live up to our true nature that God intended, but it is when we choose, out of our own free will, to fail to live up to our nature that we are 'evil' in the moral sense.

As an example, imagine you programmed Robby the robot to clean the whole house in twenty seconds flat. Provided you have programmed Robby correctly then it will indeed clean the house in the time allotted. The fact that the robot cannot write great works of poetry is not an evil, but only an absence of good, because it is not in the robot's nature (it hasn't been programmed) to write great poems. If, however, in the process of speed-cleaning, Robby's arm breaks off then it will not be able to clean the house so quickly. In this sense it is evil but not a moral evil, rather an evil in the sense of 'corrupt' (bear in mind that corrupt can mean 'rotten', 'decomposed' etc. and does not only have moral connotations). However, if you insert a 'free will chip' into Robby and, as a result, the robot decides to recline in your favourite sofa, watch television and smoke a cigarette instead of doing the cleaning then Robby has entered the realms of moral evil. He is a bad robot, but he was not *made* bad.

It is, perhaps, unfortunate that the term 'evil' had a much broader meaning in Aquinas' day than it does in ours but, leaving that aside, there are a number of problems with it:

1. Can we really blame the robot for refusing to do the cleaning or, for that matter, a human being for deciding to rob a bank? After all, it isn't the fault of you or I that we have been given free will. If God wanted us to be good, then why did He give us the freedom to refuse to do good? The belief that humans have free will is very important as a retort to the problem of evil and will be explored in more detail later in this chapter.

2. It is not altogether clear what really counts as a moral evil. It seems rather harsh to say that I am evil if I choose to be lazy today when, in actual fact, I should be striving towards my true nature. I suspect there are different levels of evil, in the same

way someone might say it's a 'crime' if someone decides to waste their potential. Of course, it isn't really a crime in the sense that a talented youngster should go to prison because he refuses to play the violin and plays video games instead; but we nonetheless might feel that it is a great shame and that we are in some way morally responsible for nurturing such a talent. Also, Aquinas' moral philosophy was based upon the principle of natural law; that by our nature we are good, but we can equally cultivate the habit of vice. Therefore, 'laziness' in itself is a vice because it is a lack of our true nature.

3. The nature versus nurture debate. It is difficult to determine what our true nature is. For example, to say that 'laziness' is a vice supposes it is our nature to pursue worthwhile goals, yet what is classed as 'worthwhile' seems more of a cultural construct.

4. What of natural evils? Volcanoes do not 'choose' to erupt, nor do oceans 'choose' to form tidal waves. Where do these evils come from? Aquinas argues that natural evil is the normal product of God's creation: it is the nature of volcanoes to erupt, of oceans to have tides, of winds to rage, of spiders to eat flies and dogs to chase after cats. Aquinas believed that, looked at from a global, objective perspective, nature *is* good because it all fits together and works. From the perspective of the fly it might seem rather harsh to be eaten by the spider, or the cat will fail to find anything good about being chased across the street by a pit- bull terrier, or the human being who is struck by lightning would hardly exclaim how good nature is. However, the workings of nature should not be see from a human-centric view, but as parts of God's intentions which, ultimately, are unknowable.

5. Aquinas was trying to show that evil is not a real 'substance' that actually has existence. If evil did have real substance then either God created it, or it exists independently of God, which would, of course, limit his omnipotence and the belief that God created everything. For something to exist at all is good: it is only the falling short of its existence that constitutes evil. In this sense, even the Devil is good; it just so happens that the Devil chooses to deny his true nature (and, after all, remember he was originally an angel). However, perhaps the most damning criticism is that arguing that evil is not a 'substance' does not alter the fact that we experience horrific acts of evil. The Holocaust was an evil, plain and simple. Saying it was an 'absence of good' does not lessen it is an evil, and nor does it explain away the fact that it occurred.

2.2 Evil is an illusion

In the USA, **Mary Baker Eddy** (1821-1910), the founder of Christian Science, believed in a system of spiritual healing based on the principle that the mind is the only reality and matter, therefore, is an illusion. Evil and suffering, being part of matter, are also illusion: "the only reality of sin, sickness and death is the awful fact that unrealities seem real to human, erring belief." In other words, what is at fault is the false belief of the sufferer that there is real suffering. For example, she claimed that a boil "simply manifests, through inflammation and swelling, a belief in pain and this belief is called a boil."

Undoubtedly, there are strong connections between the mind and the body. When someone feels depressed this can also result in physical illness. However, this is different from saying that this physical illness is not, in fact, real. As Brian Davies asks, "Can any rational person seriously hold that, say, the hunger of a starving child is simply an illusion?" Pain and suffering can be all too real, and it seems rather inhumane to dismiss the sufferings of others as a product of their own subjectivity to illusion.

3. Theodicies

In order for the theist to attempt to show that evil is compatible with a good, omnipotent God, there have been a number of theodicies (from Greek, *theo* = God: *dike* = justification). A true theodicy should:

1. Not deny the existence of evil.
2. Not qualify the nature of God.
3. Not advocate giving up belief when faced with the problem of evil.

The two great theodicies stem from the writings of St. Augustine and St. Irenaeus. Like Aquinas, both depend upon the principle of free will.

3.1 The Augustinian theodicy

Named after St Augustine (354-430), this presents the traditional biblical view of the world. That is, the world was created by God and it was 'very good' in that all of nature – including Man – was in harmony with God. However, as Adam and Eve were given free will, they used this to sin against God and the harmony was broken. In this respect, Augustine is not dissimilar from Aquinas (who, in actual fact, was influenced heavily by Augustine in developing his views on the problem of evil) in stressing the importance of free will as a determining factor and also in the belief that evil is a deprivation: it does not come from God. Even if we do not take the Bible account literally, the message remains that Man *chooses* to commit evil; it is not of God's doing.

The Augustinian theodicy, linked with Aquinas' views on evil as a deprivation, is the standard Roman Catholic view on the problem of evil. As God cannot have created evil, then its origin lies with those who have free will: angels and human beings. These have abused God's gift of freedom and so suffering is a deserved consequence of sin. All humans, even babies, deserve to suffer because all humans were present 'in the loins of Adam'. It is only through God's grace and the sending of his son to die on the cross so that we may be saved, that God shows his mercy. In fact, we all deserve to go to Hell.

There are a series of difficulties with this view that need to be addressed:

1. The theodicy does not explain why there are natural evils and nor, for that matter, why animals – who are not given free will – must also suffer. The philosopher John Stuart Mill wrote:

> "Nearly all the things which men are hanged or imprisoned for doing to one another, are Nature's everyday performance. Killing, the most criminal act, Nature does once to every being that lives!" (J.S. Mill, *Three Essays on Religion*)

Augustine's response was to explain such evils as the doings of the Devil and his gang who deliberately go around disrupting nature and causing pain to animals. However, this still does not resolve why God should see fit to *allow* the Devil to engage in such mischief. Surely by allowing the Devil to commit evil acts, God is still ultimately responsible. Alternatively, if God cannot prevent the Devil's antics, then God cannot be all-powerful. Augustine also thought that the suffering of animals was all part of the overall scheme of the harmony of nature.

2. The question remains why Adam and Eve, as well as Lucifer, should *want* to rebel against God and commit acts of evil. If the world were so harmonious and happy, then surely there would be no inclination to reject this state of affairs.

3. If God were omniscient then he would have known that Man would rebel against Him. If this is the case, then it is a fault of God's creation: Adam and Eve were not in a perfect state of

nature at all. In fact, the French Protestant theologian John Calvin (1509-1564) believed that Man's original condition was "weak, frail and liable to fall". But this vision of Man contradicts the Augustinian vision of harmonious beings created in the 'image of God'.

4. **F.D.E. Schleiermacher** (1768-1834) saw a logical contradiction with this theodicy: how could God have created a perfect world which then 'goes wrong'? Even if evil is perceived as a deprivation, it still causes suffering and, as such, this must be a part of God's making.

5. Augustine's reliance on the Genesis Creation and Fall stories are weak philosophically, as it contradicts evolutionary theory. The theological basis that we were all seminally present in Adam – and are therefore all guilty of sin – also conflicts with modern biology.

3.2 The Irenaean theodicy

This is named after St. Irenaeus (c. 120-202). Although he did not develop his thought into a theodicy as such. However, he established a framework for others to work into a theory; most notably John Hick. According to this model –which has found a home amongst many Protestant groups – humans were not in the Augustinian world of perfect harmony, but were actually created as imperfect creatures that had to develop from an animal existence to a state of awareness of God and perfection. This vision differs from the idea of the fall from grace, which pictures humanity in the Augustinian state, before 'falling' into a state of corruption, and so we can appreciate that such an idea took time to be accepted. However, Irenaeus does appeal to the Bible for support, referring to Genesis 1:26 where God said, "Let us make man in our image, after our likeness." Irenaeus took this to mean that humans were first made in God's *image* (i.e. having intelligence, morality, personality), and only later would develop into His *likeness* (i.e. completion). Man can only be 'completed' through experiencing evil and suffering.

Although God could have created Man as perfect from the beginning, human beings are not programmed robots but creatures that are free to choose or reject God. God maintains an **epistemic distance** from Man, hidden from his gaze, because if He were to appear on earth people would be so in fear that they would be immediately obedient.

Man exists in what Hick called a 'vale of soul-making'. By maintaining an epistemic distance and remaining hidden, it is hoped that Man will develop a loving relationship with God that is freely chosen and not compelled; although this does run the risk that Man, being under no compulsion, may choose to reject God.

The image of early man as spiritually and morally immature, developing into a more intelligent, ethical and religious animal, a 'child of God', is very appealing. But how can natural evil be explained? John Hick, a strong supporter of the Irenaean theodicy, argues that a world where there is no pain or suffering, where "bullets would become insubstantial when fired at a human body; poison would cease to poison; water to drown" no action would be seen as morally wrong (or, for that matter, right) and there would be no possibility of moral growth.

Hick is linking moral evil to the fact that it causes pain and suffering: if there is no pain and suffering then there is no such thing as moral evil or good. In such circumstances, humanity could not develop and mature into moral beings. In a safe, static world there would be no great challenges and exertions that aid in the growth of human personality.

However, the question that remains unanswered is why God simply didn't create complete humans in the first place. Irenaeus said that to attain the likeness of God requires the "willing co-operation of human individuals". Willing co-operation requires total freedom: we cannot willingly co-operate if we are in some way compelled to do it.

With both the Augustinian and Irenaean theodicies, as well as the thoughts of Aquinas, is that moral evil seems to occur due to human beings possessing free will. Next we need to look more closely at what the free will defence is.

4. THE FREE WILL DEFENCE

If we go back to our brief summary of the problem of evil at the beginning of this chapter:

1. God is omnipotent
2. God is omnibenevolent
3. God is omniscient
4. Evil exists

You will recall that there is an alleged inconsistency between 1-3 and 4. However, it is argued, if we were to add the following propositions then there would no longer be an inconsistency:

5. Human beings are given free will

6. The possession of free will leads to a greater good that outweighs all the evil in the world

Consequently, there is no denying that there is evil in the world, but all the evil in the world is still worth it because, by giving us free will, the good is far greater. Let's develop these two propositions further:

4.1 Human beings are given free will

In '*Evil and the God of Love*', John Hick illustrates the importance of free will:

> "The question we have to ask is not 'Is this the sort of world that an all-powerful and infinitely loving being would create as an environment for his human pets?'...The question we have to ask is rather 'Is this the kind of world that God might make as an environment in which moral beings may be fashioned, through their own insights and responses, into children of God?'" (John Hick, *Evil and the God of Love*)

As noted in the previous section, Hick, echoing the Irenaean theodicy, believed that suffering was a requirement for the human soul to develop. Hick said that faith is best understood as '**experience-as**'. For example, if you hypnotise a person so that they will love you, then you are not really experiencing true love from that person. 'Experience-as' is the kind which is hard-won rather than ready-made. Human beings are not 'pets' kept in a clean and pleasant cage, but creatures that possess souls that can progress through experience of the world. Therefore, God could prevent evil and suffering, but doing so would also mean taking away human freedom to choose to do evil because, as humans may well choose to do good they can also choose to do bad. Natural evil too, can be explained as necessary for the development of the human soul because pain and distress cannot be understood unless it is experienced.

Richard Swinburne in *The Existence of God* has further developed the free will defence. He states that a person who is completely free but, at the same time, is limited in lacking complete knowledge and awareness, can choose to either resist the temptation to do evil, or give in to it. By giving in to temptation there is the possibility that he may cause harm to himself or to others. At that point God does have the power to intervene and stop the person from committing the act, but the question is whether such an intervention would limit the person's freedom. God, being all-good, wishes to do what is best for humanity and, it is argued, allowing the person total freedom to give in to temptation – even if it results in harm – will result in that person learning from his actions and is more conducive to the development of moral autonomy.

Swinburne likens God's actions to that of a good parent who knows that too much interference will inhibit the child's own moral development. However, this brings us to proposition six in the above summary: does the good resulting in the allowance of free will outweigh the evil that results?

4.2 The possession of free will leads to a greater good that outweighs all the evil in the world

In the novel *The Brothers Karamazov* by the Russian author **Fyodor Dostoyevsky** (1821-1881), the character of Ivan discusses the problem of suffering with his brother, the priest Alyosha. Ivan provides a number of examples (taken from real accounts that Dostoyevsky had read) of atrocities committed against children. An example is given of a child who accidentally harms a dog. In response, the dog's owner sets his hounds upon the boy, tearing the child apart in front of his parents. As Ivan says, "And if the sufferings of children go to swell the sum of suffering which was necessary to pay for truth, then I protest that the truth was not worth such a price...Besides too high a price is being asked for harmony; it's beyond our means to pay so much to enter on it." You will recall Elie Wiesel at the beginning of this chapter declaring that God could not possibly exist and allow such suffering, especially that of innocent children, and of the account of the Polish guard who spoke of children being thrown into the furnace which led one Jewish writer, Irving Greenberg, to declare, "No statement, theological or otherwise, should be made that would not be credible in the presence of burning children."

To respond to this form of **protest theodicy** is not an easy thing for the defender of the existence of evil to do, and the response has often been regarded as inadequate. Eleonore Stump, for example, before presenting a defence felt compelled to say:

> "I want to suggest that Christian doctrine is committed to the claim that a child's suffering is outweighed by the

good for the child which can result from that suffering."
(Eleonore Stump, *The Problem of Evil*)

For both Stump and Hick, the problem of evil cannot be separated from the central Christian doctrine of death and life after death. As Stump relates, for the Christian, "death is not the ultimate evil or even the ultimate end, but rather a transition between one form of life and another." Rather than suggest that the suffering of the child is for some abstract general good for mankind, the Christian is committed to the belief that the child will be making a transition from a frequently painful existence in this world to a blissful and happy existence in the next world. Hick asks us to imagine a scene in heaven by which the owner of the hounds that killed the boy had been 'saved' and, as a result was ashamed and needed forgiveness for such an action. In such a case, the mother and child would forgive. This is the belief that all of us will ultimately be saved and as part of that process will be changed people and morally good.

However, such consolation – if this can be seen as consolation – seems of little significance to the billions of people who are not Christians. What fate awaits them? Stump responds to this by arguing that there is no evidence that even evil-doers will end in hell and that even those lacking the religious knowledge necessary for redemption may well, during the process of dying, be given the opportunity by God to repent. But why should the innocent, non-Christian child be *required* to repent?

A further problem is the question as to why children have to die at all. Why are they not also allowed the opportunity to grow as human beings and, therefore, develop a greater relationship and understanding of God? Again, Stump attempts to justify this by stating, "For some persons the moulding of the personality produced by suffering in infancy may be the best means of insuring a character capable of coming to God." However, it seems hardly a humane and consoling thought that the death of the child is 'good for the soul'.

5. ALTERNATIVES

If we are to avoid the severe criticisms that arise from the suffering of children, we need to see if the problem can be resolved in some other way. There are some other options, although, inevitably, they rest upon a different view to that of the God of classical theism.

5.1 God and the logically possible

If God is omnipotent then, it is argued, he can do *absolutely anything*. This would include being able to abolish all evil in the world *and* still allow Man to have free will. However, this thesis rests upon the belief that omnipotence does mean being able to do absolutely anything, including the logically impossible, such as squaring circles or God creating a being greater than Himself. Descartes was one philosopher who adopted this view of God, although – as noted in Chapter One of this book – it is not the view generally accepted as Christian doctrine. Rather, God, being perfect, would obviously not be subject to contradictions or engage in the nonsensical and so it simply does not make sense for God to make a square circle. The view that God can do the logically impossible is incoherent, and it would also mean that God could lie, deceive and commit other evils that would fly against the belief that God is all-good.

However, the atheist philosopher J.L. Mackie has argued that it is not logically impossible for God to create a world that is both devoid of suffering and allows for free will:

> "If there is no logical impossibility in a man's freely choosing the good on one, or on several occasions, there cannot be a logical impossibility of his freely choosing the good on every occasion." (J.L. Mackie, *New Essays in Philosophical Theology*)

This is a serious challenge. However, Alvin Plantinga, currently one of the leaders in the field of the philosophy of religion, believes that in every possible world that you can conceive of, a person whose nature is to be corrupt would *still be* corrupt if he was allowed the freedom to choose one or the other options (i.e. to be good or to be bad). Plantinga uses the term **transworld depravity**. By this, he means that it is human nature to suffer from depravity (that is, moral corruption) and those most subject to such depravity will eventually commit a wrong act no matter what world is conceived:

> "What is important about the idea of transworld depravity is that if a person suffers from it, then it is not within God's power to actualise any world in which that person is significantly free but does no wrong." (Alvin Pantinga, *God, Evil and the Metaphysics of Freedom*)

139

However, Mackie's claim could still hold as it is not altogether clear *why* man has to be depraved. It may well be a fact that humans are depraved in this world, but it does not necessarily follow that he has to be depraved in another possible world. Further, it does not explain why so many people have to suffer, or that we have to experience such a high degree of pain: cannot these be lessened and still have the desired effect of remaining free? More significantly, we can ask whether being logically able to always do good is really a case of man being free, and here we need to be clear about what we mean by 'freedom'.

5.2 Determinism

A key definition of determinism is that every event has a sufficient set of causes so that should those set of causes be in place the effect cannot fail to occur. For example, if I light a match and put it under some dry paper on a windless day, the paper will catch fire. Provided all the causes remain the same (the paper is dry, there is no wind to put out the match and so on), then the effect will also remain the same each time. These laws do not only apply to inanimate objects, but it is argued, also apply to animals: if you create a certain set of conditions then an animal will behave exactly as you predict. For example, if you put a cat amongst a number of pigeons then, provided the cat is hungry, healthy and does not have a phobia about pigeons, you can predict the same result each time. However, human beings are different. Humans have free will. That is, you can place a hungry person in a room full of his favourite food and he is still free to choose not to eat it. You may be able to predict that he is *likely* to eat the food, but you cannot be one hundred percent certain.

According to Descartes: "The Lord has made three marvels: things out of nothingness; free will; and the Man who is God" (*Private Thoughts*). What is interesting about this quote is the association of free will with the incarnation and the creation *ex nihilo*. That is, free will is as much a 'marvel' and a 'mystery' and, consequently, very difficult to make sense of. We intuitively consider ourselves to be free agents and, furthermore, our whole moral and legal system is based upon this very assumption: when we do something immoral we must be blamed or punished because we were free to do right. Yet what basis is there, other than our 'intuitions', for believing that we are free?

In fact, when we consider the nature of the world, there is a strong case for arguing that we are entirely determined. For example, if I am walking to work one morning and I fall onto the ground I do not simply pick myself up and say to myself, "Oh these things just happen." Rather, I would look around for an object I tripped over, some slippery substance, or go to see a doctor to explain my tendency to fall over. In other words, I will look for a relation between an effect and a cause. What I am doing is investigating the law of physics: what physical element *caused* me to fall over. Doing this, it will be possible to show that under a certain set of conditions I *had* to fall over: I would be breaking the law of physics if I didn't. It is not a sufficient explanation to say, "It just happened".

Why are human beings exempt from natural laws? As we are a part of nature it seems curious to argue that we are the only things in nature that are not determined by the laws of nature! In addition, if we are suggesting that when we do things the laws of nature, biology, or even psychology cannot explain it, then how are we to make sense of ourselves? Do the things that we do 'just happen'? Undoubtedly we are more complex than other animals, but the problem lies in the *complexity* of causes rather than to say that we are not caused. Referring to the earlier example of the hungry man in the room full of food, the determinist would argue that his unwillingness to eat the food still has causal connections but they are considerably more complex and varied than that of a cat. The belief that we are free agents is actually nothing more than an illusion.

There are still unresolved problems with determinism. Much contemporary science, notably quantum theory, argues that laws are not as deterministic as originally thought. However, this is still highly speculative and it is quite possible that it is merely a case that we have not found sufficient causes at the micro level yet, rather than that there aren't any. Nonetheless, the so-called **libertarian** maintains that there are such things as free acts: that is acts that are uncaused. Yet this raises its own problems that are not so dissimilar from determinism, especially in terms of moral agency. In the same way it might be argued that if we are determined then we are not responsible for our actions, likewise if there are no causes for our actions then we are also not responsible. For example, if I throw a custard pie into someone's face I can simply say, "I didn't cause it."

5.3 Compatibilism (or soft determinism)
When a youngster commits a crime and he goes to court it is usual to take account of the child's upbringing. If it turns out that the child was physically and mentally abused by his parents, was

starved of emotion and food, and so on, then these environmental conditions are taken into account when passing sentence. *Why?* Why not simply say that the child could have freely chosen to ignore the temptation to steal but, because he didn't, he should be severely punished? This is a case where the child is not considered to be entirely to blame for his actions. In other words, he was not truly free but a 'product' of the conditions that he was brought up in. This is not to say that all children brought up in the same conditions (and arguably, no two conditions are the same anyway) would also commit crimes, but rather that, in this case, the stealing may be seen as a cry for attention, or an act of desperation, rather than a calculated choice to commit a crime

Another example is that provided by Anthony Flew, in *New Essays in Philosophical Theology*. Here we have the case of a person called Murdo who chooses to marry Mairi:

> "To say that Murdo was free to ask whichever eligible girl of his acquaintance he wanted, and that he chose to ask, was accepted by, and has now married Mairi of his own free will, is not to say that his actions and choices were uncaused or in principle unpredictable." (A. Flew, *New Essays in Philosophical Theology*)

The point here is that we *seem* to have freedom of action in the sense that there are options presented to us, but we are in a way still conditioned to lean towards one option rather than another, even though we are still exercising our 'free will'. In this sense the act is both 'free' and determined at the same time: all actions have a sufficient set of causes, but sometimes the agent's will is the primary cause of the action. It is this kind of freedom that Mackie meant when he said that it is logically possible for people to always 'lean towards' the good actions whilst still be presented with the choice to do bad.

However, problems remain with compatibilism, especially when we start talking of an agent's 'will'. Where does this will come from? Isn't it a product of our biology, our genetics and culture? In which case, is not our will also determined?

5.4 Process theodicy

Process theodicy was developed by the British philosopher **A.N. Whitehead** (1861-1947). This view of God does not see Him as some omnipotent, distant and immutable (unchangeable) entity, but rather in a more 'human' sense as a being that reacts and responds to the actions of man. Again, the parent analogy is appropriate here. The parent is the creator of the child and is there to guide and persuade, but does not have complete control over the child's actions, especially as the infant grows. Also the parent can be hurt by what the sibling does and says. In this sense, God, like the parent, is also in the process of developing and learning and is thus affected by the universe, as well as affecting it. This view of God is what is known as **panentheism**.

Although there would no longer be a problem of evil, this view of God is far removed from the God of classical theism, and would be unacceptable for many traditional Christians. In fact, it could be argued that this is not really a theodicy at all for it does not justify the existence of God in the face of evil but actually removes the concept of an omnipotent God. The possibility has been considered that God created the universe as a finely balanced system that, if He were to interfere in its operation, would cause too much disharmony. In this respect, the laws of nature could limit God, although it still raises the question *why* God would wish to limit Himself this way.

5.5 Evil is the will of God

One way of maintaining God's omnipotence is to say that he *could* prevent evil, but chooses not to. God creates some people for an eternal life, while others are created for a destiny in hell. The Protestant reformer **John Calvin** (1509-1564) taught that all men are not created equal: some are destined for heaven, while others for eternal damnation.

However, this theodicy has obvious weaknesses. If man is thus predestined he cannot be held responsible for his actions. Also, it does not resolve the problem of the suffering of children. As Peter Vardy stresses, "God does not want suffering, he does not will evil, he does not use suffering as a means to some wider end" (*The Puzzle of Evil,* p.119). To suggest that God selects some for eternal life and some for eternal damnation based purely on some wider, abstract goal, and entirely separate from the life the person leads, does seem to present a less than perfect God, an "obscene God" in Vardy's words.

5.6 The Devil made me do it

St. Augustine developed his theodicy partly as a response to the teachings of the sect known as **Manicheism**. Augustine himself was a Manichean for nine years before converting to Christianity. The Manicheans were founded by the Persian prophet Mani in the third century and they taught that the world consisted of a physical dualism of good power and evil power: the realm of light (spirit), ruled over by God, and the realm of Darkness (matter), ruled by Satan. As humans are made of matter, they are essentially evil, although they possess a soul, which is a remnant of the realm of light. Therefore, humans can be redeemed through knowledge of the realm of light that has been imparted by such prophets as the Buddha, Jesus and Mani himself.

Such teaching goes against that of both Augustus and Aquinas who believed that evil was not a substance at all. In 563 AD the Council of Braga declared Manicheism a heresy and laid down the doctrine that Satan was created by God and had become sinful through the exercise of his own free will. This was important, as to suggest that there is an evil force that existed separate from God would limit God's omnipotence. These days, of course, many Christians deny the existence of Satan at all and prefer to see the Devil as a metaphor for evil, although the idea of powerful forces of evil that can cajole and persuade man is a powerful one that still can be seen through more modern media such as the cinema: Darth Vader in *Star Wars* is a prime example.

Aquinas, following the line of Aristotle, believed that good is, 'that to which all desire ends.' God, therefore, is the archetype of goodness; to worship God is to desire Good. As God is the goal of all creation (for God is creation), then so is the Good. Yet many find evil – to different degrees – more attractive: Milton's Satan is far more charismatic than the squeaky clean God. Having said that, however, deep down many of us believe that the best world is one where there is no evil or suffering, yet we are afraid of existing in some kind of Brave New World, devoid of passion. How far are we prepared to go to avoid the pains that seem such a part of life?

As Peter Vardy explains:

> "The position that traditional Christianity has always maintained is that the world is not wholly in God's control because it is in the grip of transcendent forces that are dependent on God for their existence but have used their God-given freedom to rebel against God." (Peter Vardy, *The Puzzle of Evil*)

This view maintains God's omnipotence in that the universe is still dependent upon God for its existence, yet also rests the responsibility for evil upon the shoulders of people who have God-given free will. Evil is a force to be reckoned with, but its very existence is dependent upon humanity's willingness to be subject to it.

Further reading

Augustine, *City of God*, Doubleday, 1958.

Aquinas, T, *Summa Theologica*, Eyre & Spottiswoode, 1964.

Davies, Brian, *An Introduction to the Philosophy of Religion*, OUP, 1993. (Chap. 3)

Flew, A. & A. McIntyre, *New Essays in Philosophical Theology*, SCM, 1955.

Helm, Paul, *The Providence of God*, IVP, 1979.

Hick, John, *Evil and the God of Love*, Collins, 1968.

Lewis, C.S. *The Great Divorce*, Fontana, 1972.

Le Poidevin, Robin, *Arguing for Atheism,* Routledge, 1996. (Chap. 7)

Mill, J.S., *The Problem of Evil*, in 'The Existence of God' ed. by John Hick, Macmillan, 1964.

Mackie, J.L., *Evil and Omnipotence*, in 'The Philosophy of Religion' ed. by Basil Mitchell, OUP, 1971. (Chap. 5)

Plantinga, Alvin, *The Free Will Defence*, in 'The Philosophy of Religion' ed. by Basil Mitchell, OUP, 1971. (Chap. 6)

Quinn, Philip L. and Charles Taliaferro (ed), *A Companion to Philosophy of Religion*, Blackwell, 1999. (Chap. 50)

Stump, Eleanor & Michael J. Murray (ed), *Philosophy of Religion: The Big Questions*, Blackwell, 1999. (Part 3)

Swinburne, Richard, *The Existence of God,* Clarendon Press, 1979.

Thompson, Mel, *Teach Yourself Philosophy of Religion,* Hodder & Stoughton, 1997. (Chap. 7)

Vardy, Peter, *The Puzzle of Evil*, Fount, 1992.

Chapter Eleven
LIFE AFTER DEATH

"Friends, I can't persuade Crito that I am Socrates here, the one who is now conversing and arranging each of the things being discussed; but he imagines I'm that dead body he'll see in a little while, so he goes and asks how he's to bury me! But as for the great case I've been arguing all this time, that when I drink the poison, I shall no longer remain with you, but shall go off and depart for some happy state of the blessed, this, I think, I'm putting to him in vain, while comforting you and myself alike."

(Plato, *Phaedo*)

Fundamental to most religions is the doctrine of life after death. Certainly, if it can be shown that there is life after death then this would help count towards any argument for the existence of God. At the very least, it would raise questions concerning natural empirical laws or the view that there is nothing 'out there'. Coupled with the belief in life after death is the question of what it is that continues after death? Talk is often of the continuance of the 'soul' and even many who are not religious intuitively feel that they have a 'soul' or 'mind' of some kind and are not mere machines.

1. How Can We Survive Death? The Mind-Body Problem
1.1 Dualism

The dualist approach is that there exist both a body and a mind that are distinct from each other, but also in some way interlinked. The body is the 'material' and, as such, is tied to the limitations that the world of matter is subject to, such as ageing and decay and, of course, eventually death. The mind, however, is not part of the temporal, changeable world and so is usually considered eternal and spaceless.

Plato

The Greek word for soul is 'psyche', which suffers somewhat in translation. A better translation would be 'life force' or 'life principle' as this lacks the religious connotations that it now possesses. Our main source for Plato's views on the soul can be found in his *Phaedo*. In this book Socrates is in prison shortly before his execution. He is having a conversation with some friends and it is perhaps natural on such an occasion that he should speculate upon the nature of life after death and the eternal soul.

Socrates explains that the true philosopher should look forward to death and that they should therefore ready themselves for dying. Plato's views on life after death are closely connected with his theory of the Forms, because it is in the realm of the Forms that the soul resides when not tied to the body. As the physical world is transient and illusory, the philosopher should surely wish to escape the distractions of the body and the world around him so as to dwell in the realm of pure intellect. The body and all its weaknesses – the desire for food, sensuous satisfaction, and illness – is perceived as a hindrance towards the mental pursuit of truth. The philosopher, in order to attain knowledge of the Forms, is in a constant struggle with the world of the senses.

To battle against the senses it is necessary to continually engage in **katharsis.** This Greek word has come down to us in English as 'catharsis', which usually means to relieve an emotional or neurotic condition by relating a traumatic experience that has been repressed. Katharsis, for Plato, was a form of purification. Plato was greatly influence by a mystic group known as the Pythagoreans, who practised a form of regular purification of the body by using types of herbal medicines, fasting, and engaging in music, dance and song. By means of various austere practices Plato believed you could become aware of the delusion of material gain and sensuous pleasures and instead focus upon the Forms, which, in effect, brings you closer to death. In death, the soul is released from the body and so is no longer subject to bodily distractions. In such a case why should the philosopher fear death?

The soul, Plato believes, is eternal. At the death of the body the soul continues in a disembodied existence as pure intellect, residing within the realm of the Forms. However, once freed from the body, the soul is weighed down by the corruption of the sensual world. If the person who dies has lived an evil life, then the soul will be reborn as a lower animal such as an ass. However, if you have lived a virtuous life then you will be reborn as a better human being. Ultimately, the further you escape from the pleasure of the sensual world the more likely it is that the soul will remain in the realm of the Forms.

Aristotle

Aristotle also talked of the 'psyche', but adopts a less dualistic approach than Plato. For Aristotle all living things, from prawns to daffodils, possess souls, because the soul, the 'animator', by definition gives life to a living thing. However, these souls differ in their complexity.

What distinguishes Aristotle's soul from Plato's is that the soul is not a separate thing from the body, and nor is it some spiritual substance that resides inside the physical body. Rather, it is a set of 'powers' or faculties. Plants, for example, only possess the basic power of the soul of nutrition, whereas animals possess nutrition, perception, appetite, and motion. Human beings also possess the power of thought.

> "Possessing a soul is like possessing a skill. A carpenter's skill is not some part of him, responsible for his skilled acts; similarly, a living creature's animator or soul is not some part of it, responsible for its living activities."
> (Jonathan Barnes, *Aristotle: A Very Short Introduction*)

Therefore, the soul is the fulfilment of the body and so the soul cannot exist separately from the body in the same way a person's skill in carpentry cannot cannot exist separately from the person. He also thought it was as absurd to believe that the soul enters the body from outside as it is to believe your feet can attach themselves to your body from outside.

Aristotle, therefore, adopts a much more material approach to the soul, although the question remains as to why we need to talk of a 'soul' or 'animator' at all instead of simply saying that the body has certain functions. Further, Aristotle does drift away from a material explanation of the soul when talking of the power of thought that humans possess. In *De Anima* he says,

> "Hence it remains that thought alone comes in from outside, and that it alone is divine; for corporeal actuality has no connection at all with the actuality of thought."

Thought, therefore, can exist separately from the body. What he meant by 'thought' here is unclear, although he seems to be referring to it in the most abstract sense of pure reason that has no connection with memories or personality.

Aquinas

Following on from Aristotle, Aquinas referred to the soul as the '*anima*'; that which animates the body; that gives it life force:

> "Now that the soul is what makes our body live; so the soul is the primary source of all these activities that differentiate levels of life: growth, sensation, movement, understanding mind or soul, it is the form of our body." (Thomas Aquinas, *Summa Theologica*)

However, Aquinas differed from Aristotle in the belief that the soul completely survives death with its own individual identity (memories, personality and so on). This is far removed from Aristotle's abstract universal 'intellect' and is also a departure from the early Christian beliefs, which argue for the resurrection of the whole body.

Descartes

Descartes attempted to address the crucial question of where such phenomena as thought, feelings and so on come from. If we are to adopt the view that all that exists is matter then matter does not contain within it such things as emotion or reasoning. Where, therefore, do these kind of phenomena come from? This led to what is referred to as **Cartesian dualism** ('Cartesian' is the adjective formed from the name 'Descartes'), or **substance dualism.** Descartes considered the separate properties (characteristics) that the mind and body possess:

Body	Mind
Has material substance (has size, shape, weight, position, movement)	Has non-corporeal substance (no size, shape, weight, position, movement)
Exists in space (has length, breadth, depth)	Spaceless (no length, breadth, depth)
Exists in time (changes, ages, decays and dies)	Timeless (does not change, age, decay or die)
Performs physical activities	Pure consciousness
Separate from mind	Separate from body

Descartes believed that our identity, our 'I', comes from our mind, and so our body is largely irrelevant to who we are:

> "Our soul is of a nature entirely independent of the body, and consequently…it is not bound to die with it. And since we cannot see any other causes which destroy the soul, we are naturally led to conclude that it is immortal." (René Descartes, *Discourse on Method*)

For Descartes, then, the soul is eternal and, upon the death of the body, resides with God. The problem, however, is how can two so very different things such as the body and soul (or mind) possibly co-exist and act upon each other? Descartes put forward the view that has become known as **interactionism**. This holds that mind and body interact in the sense that the state of mind can affect the bodily state (for example, you feel angry and this results in you banging your fist on the table) and, likewise, states of the body can affect states of the mind (you eat ice-cream and it causes you to reflect upon your childhood). Indeed, Descartes went further and located the point that the two interact in the pineal gland.

However, Descartes had to confess that he could not explain *how* two such very different phenomena could possibly interact. You have no doubt seen many movies and TV programmes where someone dies and comes back as a ghost. One of the first problems the ghost encounters is that he is unable to grab door handles and so soon learns that he can simply walk through doors. This is the same problem with interactionism: the mind is non-spatial and yet can affect and be affected by the spatial. How is this possible? How, for example, can the drinking of alcohol possibly affect the mind?

This problem has led various dualists to present alternatives. **Parallelism** denies that there is any interaction. Leibniz, who argued that the mind and body only *seem* to be interacting (one having an actual affect upon the other) but are really working in parallel, presented one version of this. The best way to imagine this is to conceive of two clocks that are both synchronised to the same time: one clock has a clock-face, with hands but no alarm bell. The other clock has an alarm bell, but no clock-face. However, they are both set so that when one clock hand reaches the hour, the other clock alarm goes off. In this sense, they appear to be linked in some way, but in actual fact they are not. The mind and body work in a similar way. What regulates them? For

Leibniz, the answer lies with God. When someone stabs me with a pin I feel pain and anger, but not because my body sent a message to my mind that I have been stabbed by a pin; rather God had set these events on a pre-ordained course.

Apart from the fact that it assumes that God exists, there are other serious problems with parallelism. Firstly, it presents difficulties in terms of free will. If everything is pre-determined, if all events run like clockwork, then we are not free agents in any way. This raises theological and philosophical difficulties that were discussed in Chapter Ten. Secondly, modern science has shown that there *are* links between the mind and the brain. In particular, the evidence presented by the 'split-brain' cases of the 1960s. As a way of treating severe epilepsy, surgeons cut the fibres that link the two hemispheres of the brain. This – upon reflection – somewhat unwise procedure resulted in a serious side-effect as it created two 'minds'. The right hemisphere of the brain gets its information from the left side of the visual field, whereas the left hemisphere gets its information from the right side. In the case of split-brain patients, the two hemispheres could no longer interact so that the left side could only identify what existed on the right side of the patient's visual field, and vice versa. The supporter of parallelism might attempt to argue that this is simply the mind still working in parallel with the body, but the argument does seem seriously weakened.

Another theory worthy of a brief mention here is **occasionalism**, which – unlike parallelism – argues that there really is a link between the mind and body, but this interaction is caused by the working of God. However, it still suffers from the same criticism that it relies on the existence of God and brings into question free will.

Epiphenomenalism is particularly associated with the English zoologist **T.H. Huxley** (1825-1895) – the man who originally coined the term 'agnostic' - and does at least accommodate the split-brain thesis more comfortably than parallelism. Epiphenomenalism states that mental events *are* the effects of physical events. However, it cannot work the other way around: mental events cannot cause physical events. Rather the mind is a by-product of physical events rather like your shadow is a by-product of you. The mental is 'above' (*epi*) the processes of brain events. This view seems to go against our intuitions: I decide to walk to the library, and this is what makes me begin my walk to the library. For the epiphenomenalist, this intuition is an illusion: the mental decision is not what causes me to start walking.

However, we are still faced with the problem of free will. I can never think of doing something and then go ahead and do it. Rather I am merely some automaton that simply 'does' things and is under the illusion that I did them according to my own volition. Further, the theory does not address the issue as to why or how physical events can affect mental events, but not the other way around.

It seems that the problems with dualism strike many fatal blows. Even if it were conceivable that the soul can in some way interact with the body, this does not therefore lead to the conclusion that the soul is eternal. Perhaps the soul is more like Aristotle's psyche: a life-force, or 'animator' that essentially dies with the body. Many modern dualists are **property dualists**, which comes close to the Aristotlein view. Property dualists hold that there is only the complete person that has both physical properties and mental properties. These two properties are not identical in nature, yet neither are they separate substances and the mind cannot survive without the body. However, this still has problems; as with Aristotle it is difficult to appreciate why there is the need for a mental property at all, and nor does it really help to identify what the mental actually consists of in terms of substance, or how it interacts with the rest of the body. In a sense this is not really 'dualism' as classically understood, and is sometimes referred to as **soft materialism** to distinguish it from the 'harder' kind that is described below.

1.2 Materialism

Supporters of materialism (also known as **physicalism**) believe that there is no such substance as a 'soul' or 'mind'. Rather, the human being is made up of matter and nothing more. Consequently, at death the body decays and the person, the 'I', ceases to exist.

Gilbert Ryle

The English philosopher Gilbert Ryle (1900-76) described the idea of the soul as "the ghost in the machine" in his work *The Concept of Mind* (1949). This work Ryle himself described as "a sustained piece of analytical hatchet-work" on Cartesian dualism. Ryle believed that dualism was a **category mistake**; a mistake in the way we use language. The result is that people speak of the mind and the body as different substances as if the soul is something identifiably distinct from the body, rather like saying the British Constitution is some shadowy being which exists separate from the Cabinet, Opposition, and other institutions of Parliament. Ryle gives the example of a foreign visitor to a university who is shown the colleges, the library, the staff area, the science labs, and so on. At the end of the tour, the visitor asks, "Where is the university?" Another example Ryle provides is of someone who watches a game of cricket and asks, "Where is the team spirit?" as if this is something separate from the umpire, players and fans.

For Ryle, any talk of a soul is really a way of describing the way someone acts or behaves. For example, some people laugh at things that others find sad, some get angry over things that others are unconcerned about, some fall in and out of love easily while others love one person for life. These are all behavioural characteristics that distinguish one person from another. But this is not the same as saying that each possesses a unique soul. This view is known as **logical behaviourism**: if I were to say that I desire ice-cream this, for Ryle, is merely the disposition to soon perform 'having an ice cream behaviour'. There is no mind that contains desires and beliefs on the topic of ice-cream, just dispositions to behave in certain ways.

When we talk of people having 'beliefs', Ryle substitutes this with 'dispositions'. Ryle gives the example of a lake that has frozen over. In this example, the person's 'belief' that the ice is thin is his or her 'disposition' to tell others that it is thin, to skate warily on it, and so on. In the same way, when we describe someone as 'polite' we are not describing a part of his mind but saying he displays polite behaviour such as holding the door open for others.

There are various objections to this theory. Firstly, if we go back to the thin ice example, how can Ryle account for the fact that someone might, while believing the ice to be thin, actually be disposed not to tell anyone or choose to skate dangerously because he or she has a death-wish? Ryle, however, does take account of the fact that people deceive others and themselves but, he believes, this would not weaken his theory, rather it merely shows that certain people have a disposition to lie or that 'wishing' to die is another way of describing behaviour. However, a second and stronger criticism is that when I say 'I feel pain' I am not referring to my own behaviour but to a sensation. That is, behaviourism does not take account of **qualia** – the feeling that experiences have for the person who has them. A third point is that not all mind states are expressed as behaviour states. For example, one person may actually be in pain while another is acting as if he is in pain while in actual fact feeling rather happy: both display the same behaviour, but their mental states differ.

Identity theory

Another form of materialism is **identity theory.** Like logical behaviourism, this theory holds that mind states are actually physical states, but differs in that it does not explain these states as 'dispositions'. Rather, every event that occurs has a full physical cause, although we give two descriptions for something that is actually one. For example, the term 'water' and 'H_2O' are a way of identifying the same thing. However, both terms have slightly different meanings and are related to the linguistic context we are operating within. That is, if I wanted a glass of water it would be rather strange to ask for a glass of 'H_2O'. However, if I wanted to explain the chemical composition of water, then using the term 'H_2O' would be quite appropriate. In the same way, 'a recollection of my childhood' and 'a physical brain state' is actually the same thing; however, it would be strange for me to say 'I'm having a physical brain state' in everyday conversation any more than I would ask for a glass of H_2O.

Again, there are problems related to this theory. Although it opens the door for the neuropsychologists to find material the source for our mental states, it does not alter the fact that – at present at least – they don't *have* the source. We *know* our mental states, but we do not know what physical states these supposedly relate to. However, this objection may be overcome in time if neuropsychologists are able to identify every single thought to a particular brain process. But will this really ever be possible? Again, identity theory seems to dismiss *qualia* too readily, as we are not dealing with inanimate objects when we talk of thoughts and feelings.

John Hick's replica theory

It has, up to now, been argued that materialists believe that there is no mind or soul and that, therefore, when the material body dies then so does the 'self'. However, it was noted earlier that early Christianity did not argue for a separate soul, but that the whole body would be resurrected after death. In this sense, it is a form of materialism, although what would be the actual 'material' of what St. Paul describes as the 'spiritual' body remains unclear.

The problem with such a view is that it is clear to our senses that the body, upon death, does begin to decay until, eventually, all that is left is the skeleton. How then can the resurrected person be the same individual as he or she was before death?

John Hick has argued that it would be possible for the physical body to continue to exist after death as the same person if an exact replica of them were to appear. This is known as Hick's **replica theory**. Hick explains this theory by means of a thought experiment. He imagined a man called John Smith who lived in the United States. One day Smith suddenly vanishes in front of his friends and, at that same instant, a replica 'Smith' appeared in India. This replica is exactly the same as the person who disappeared in America, both physically and mentally. He has all the same emotions and memories. The replica also considers himself to be John Smith, not a copy. Hick argues that, in time, his friends would accept that this is in fact John Smith, despite the miraculous disappearance and re-appearance

Hick is arguing that it is reasonable and *logically possible* to accept that the person who disappeared in the United States and re-appeared in India is the same person. In the same way, suppose John Smith dies and God created him in the next world in that same instant. This would also be the same person. He would continue to exist as a resurrection replica in a resurrection world. This 'resurrection world' exists completely separately from our own earthly existence.

However, Hick depends on the view that because it is logically possible for there to be a replica of John Smith, then it is reasonable to assume this to actually be possible. However, it may be logically possible for me to marry the most beautiful woman in the world, but this does not make it *actually* possible.

Secondly, Brian Davies has presented his own thought experiment. Davies asks us to imagine that you are given a lethal dose of poison. Would you be consoled into accepting the poison if you are told that a replica of you will appear the instant you die? As Davies also points out, a replica of a Turner or a Rembrandt is still only a *replica*.

One final criticism is, of course, that Hick does rely on the existence of God and to respond to the question of how it is possible that a replica can appear in a resurrection world by saying 'God can do anything' lacks philosophical rigour.

2. EVIDENCE FOR LIFE AFTER DEATH
2.1 Near-death experiences (NDEs)

Due to advances in medical technology more and more people have been resuscitated after being clinically 'dead'. Of course, these people are not actually dead as, by definition, this is the point of no return. However, they are near death in the sense that they have no heartbeat and, in some cases, no brain activity either. Dr. Raymond Moody coined the phrase 'near-death experience' (NDE) in his book *Life After Death* (1975) to describe the experiences of some people who have been resuscitated. When asked for descriptions of what they experienced whilst being near death, Moody noted that they typically share certain similar features:

- Firstly, the individual feels a sense of peace and well-being
- Secondly, the patient undergoes an out-of-body experience (OBE), a feeling of being outside the body and floating above it.
- From this vantage point the patient is able to observe the events below
- The patient is then drawn into darkness, a rapid movement down a tunnel with a bright light at the end
- Upon entering this light, there is a feeling of being enveloped by it and a sense of being in the presence of a divine being, and sometimes there are dead relatives and friends with whom the patient can communicate with telepathically
- There often follows a 'life review' or 'panoramic recall' in which the individual is shown a view of their own life, its effect on others, and to see themselves as they really are
- The next stage involves a view of a heavenly realm of beauty and peace (although in some cases this is a hellish realm of fire and fear)
- Finally, the patient reaches a barrier – a wall or a bridge – and decides or is told whether or not to return to their physical bodies. At this point the patient 'wakes up'.

These set of experiences are used as evidence that a soul can exist outside of the confines of the body. Adherents point to the commonality of the experience as proof that there is life after death. However this commonality has been questioned. Carol Zaleski in her work *Otherworld Journeys* (1988) researched cases of medieval NDEs. These accounts described subjects being eaten by dragons and attacked by serpents and toads, as well as 'test bridges' where the person had to pass various ordeals to cross them. The fact that these accounts differ so much from modern accounts suggest a cultural reference, rather than a universal experience. However, like religious experiences, the explanation for this may be that the subject is bound to interpret events within their own cultural boundaries, although this does not deny the fact that something actually did occur.

Other naturalistic explanations have been given for the various characteristics of NDEs. For example, a change of blood pressure can evoke a floating sensation, whilst a reduction in oxygen to the brain can lead to hallucinations. However, airplane pilots that have lost oxygen do not experience NDEs or are able to give such clear and coherent accounts of their hallucinations. The OBEs, it has been argued, could merely be the effect of apparently looking from above as a recreation from your memory, whereas providing an account of what the doctors are doing to the subject during this time could be due to having seen medical programmes on TV. The experience of travelling through a tunnel with a bright light at the end might be some dim memory of travelling through the birth canal.

2.2 Ghosts

Sightings of ghosts are not uncommon. The question, however, is whether what people claim to see really is a ghost or whether they can be explained by naturalistic means. One possibility is that it is a result of elaborate tricks or hoaxes. Alternatively, the power of suggestion could lead to the mistaken belief that a ghost has been seen. What is more difficult to explain is that ghosts are sometimes reported to be seen by more than one person at a time and that certain places seem to have more sightings of ghosts than others.

2.3 Psychic evidence

Spiritualism involves communication between the spirit world and the world of the living usually through 'mediums' that pass on messages from the dead containing information that the medium would not have known. Many mediums have been shown to be frauds, but by no means all. Many are sceptical of this method because of the particular vulnerability of the participants: as they are usually people who seek comfort from their dead loved ones they are more likely to believe that they are communicating with the dead. Evidence one way or the other is still inconclusive.

Telepathy is when a thought can be 'picked up' by another person without the aid of normal communication. In terms of life after death, it is believed that if it can be shown that there is such a thing as ESP (extra-sensory perception), then it points to the possibility that the world is not simply material, but that there is a non-physical element and would, therefore, provide stronger evidence for the existence of spirits or a soul. Research here is also still very inconclusive and, even if it can be shown that some have a tendency towards ESP this in itself is not evidence that there is life after death as there could still be a material, naturalistic explanation.

Psychokinesis is the ability to move objects with the mind. There have been various recorded experiences of psychokinesis. For example, the Russian housewife, Nelya Mikhailova, who, through psychokinesis, seemed to separate the yolk of an egg from its white. More recently, Uri Geller made quite a successful living out of seemingly bending spoons with his mind. Again, even if it is shown that some people have such ability there could still be a scientific explanation for this. There is much we still do not know about the power of the brain and the fact that we use such a small percentage of it indicates that it may have considerably more latent power than we are currently aware of.

2.4 Past lives

Under hypnosis, people have recounted past lives. This may provide evidence that, at death, the soul takes on a new identity. Under hypnosis, the subjects have taken on different personalities, voices and even spoken in different languages. Some of these memories have been very accurate accounts of people and places from the past, with details that were confirmed only after historical investigation. However, this information could have been acquired by reading historical documents, watching a documentary on TV, and so on, although there do seem to be some accounts that were only discovered to be true by new historical discoveries.

This view of life after death presents the continued existence of memory which many believers in **reincarnation** would not accept. In reincarnation the 'soul' lives a different life in a different body and the memories of previous lives are usually considered non-existent. In certain varieties of Buddhism there is a denial that there is a 'soul' as such or an 'I', a personal identity, that continues in the next life. Nonetheless, Tibetan Buddhism, for example, relies upon the continued existence of personal identity to detect the rebirth of the Dalai Lama in another body. For example, the child may 'recall' objects that belonged to his previous life.

Further reading

Churchland, Paul, *Matter and Consciousness,* MIT Press, 1988.

Davies, Brian, *An Introduction to the Philosophy of Religion,* OUP, 1993. (Chap. 11)

Quinn, Philip L. and Charles Taliaferro, *A Companion to Philosophy of Religion,* Blackwell, 1999. (Chap. 70)

Searle, John, *Minds, Brains and Science,* Penguin, 1989.

Stump, Eleanor & Michael J. Murray (ed), *Philosophy of Religion: The Big Questions,* Blackwell, 1999. (Chaps.41-43)

Thompson, Mel, *Teach Yourself Philosophy of Religion,* Hodder & Stoughton, 1997. (Chap. 5)

Vardy, Peter, *The Puzzle of God,* Fount, 1999. (Chap. 18)